Johannes Schumann

# Englisch *ganz leicht*

## Rätsel & Übungen

für zwischendurch

Hueber Verlag

5. 4. 3. | Die letzten Ziffern
2011 10 09 08 07 | bezeichnen Zahl und Jahr des Druckes.
Alle Drucke dieser Auflage können, da unverändert,
nebeneinander benutzt werden.
1. Auflage

Umschlaggestaltung: Parzhuber und Partner, München
Zeichnungen: Tatiana Žitňanová, Bratislava, Slowakei
Layout: Petra Obermeier, München
Druck und Bindung: Ludwig Auer GmbH, Donauwörth
Printed in Germany
ISBN 978-3-19-007908-7

## Vorwort

Wie oft hat man nicht zwischendurch mal ein paar Minuten Zeit zum Lernen! Im Bus, am Strand, im Café ... Nutzen Sie diese Zeit zum Wiederholen und Entdecken von Neuem. Mit *Englisch ganz leicht Rätsel und Übungen für zwischendurch* können Sie Ihren Grundwortschatz festigen und erweitern – eben auf ganz leichte Art! Dieses Buch bietet Ihnen 100 abwechslungsreiche Rätsel und Übungen (im Folgenden „Tests" genannt) zu verschiedenen Themenbereichen. Die Lösungen im Anhang geben Ihnen die nötige Sicherheit und Kontrolle.

Denken Sie daran, dass es nicht wichtig ist, möglichst viele Tests hintereinander zu lösen. Prägen Sie sich jeweils nur einen Test gut ein – aber möglichst regelmäßig und am besten täglich. Markieren Sie, was Ihnen wichtig ist und was Sie lernen möchten.
Beim Wortschatzerwerb spielt die Häufigkeit der Wiederholung die entscheidende Rolle, damit Neues ins Langzeitgedächtnis übergehen kann.

Dieses Testbuch ist geeignet für erwachsene Selbstlerner, aber auch für Schüler, die in abwechslungsreicher und spielerischer Form ihre Sprachkenntnisse auffrischen wollen.

Wir wünschen Ihnen viel Spaß!

## DIESE ARTEN VON TESTS GIBT ES



Hinweis: Einige Testnummern sind unter mehreren Rubriken genannt.

## TESTS ZU BESTIMMTEN THEMEN



## TESTS ZU WORTSCHATZ UND GRAMMATIK

## TEST 1 Setzen Sie ein.

aloud application at be ~~cross~~ different duty fond German haircut map only pick pieces possible result send special travel work

1. den Fluss überqueren > to cross the river
2. laut lesen > to read ________
3. ich hole dich ab > I'll ________ you up
4. schwer arbeiten > to ________ hard
5. gern haben / lieb haben > to be ________ of / to like
6. verschieden sein > to be ________
7. Besten Dank für Ihre Bewerbung. > We thank you for your ________.
8. sich die Haare schneiden lassen > to have a ______
9. nichts Besonderes > nothing ________
10. mit dem Schiff fahren > to ________ by ship
11. Bitte zeigen Sie mir das auf der Karte. > Please show it to me on the ____.
12. im Hotel übernachten > to stay ____ the hotel
13. in Stücke schneiden > to cut into ________
14. ins Deutsche übersetzen > to translate into ________
15. so bald wie möglich > as soon as ________
16. holen lassen / kommen lassen > to ________ for
17. erst gestern > ________ yesterday
18. es ist meine Pflicht zu > it's my ________ to
19. es wird schon werden / gehen > it will ____ all right
20. zur Folge haben > to ________ in

## Was passt links und rechts zusammen?

| | | |
|---|---|---|
| 1. | flower | sugar |
| 2. | car | lid |
| 3. | train | ticket |
| 4. | coffee | vase |
| 5. | pot | boot / trunk |

| | | |
|---|---|---|
| a) | soup | ski lift |
| b) | fever | mustard |
| c) | stairs | banisters |
| d) | sausage | thermometer |
| e) | snow | spoon |

| | | |
|---|---|---|
| I. | bicycle | stage |
| II. | theatre | clown |
| III. | pub | beer |
| IV. | circus | leather |
| V. | jacket | bell |

| | | |
|---|---|---|
| A) | zoo | music |
| B) | computer | star |
| C) | sky | animals |
| D) | disco | suitcase |
| E) | luggage | printer |

## TEST 3 Finden Sie Wortpaare mit gegenteiliger Bedeutung.

blunt ~~boring~~ bottom dirty down dry early empty happy light never old opaque poor rough rude short stale wrong young

1. interesting - boring
2. tall - ____________
3. rich - ____________
4. sad - ____________
5. new - ____________
6. smooth - ____________
7. sharp - ____________
8. clean - ____________
9. up - ____________
10. top - ____________
11. fresh - ____________
12. late - ____________
13. wet - ____________
14. old - ____________
15. full - ____________
16. right - ____________
17. transparent - ____________
18. always - ____________
19. heavy - ____________
20. polite - ____________

**Setzen Sie ein.**



beginning Can Follow Keep listening money next ~~piece~~ quite receipt recommended taste test town tree Turn understand upset windshield

1. Was für ein Glück! > What a __piece__ of good luck!
2. Das ist eine gute Gelegenheit, Geld zu verdienen. > This is a good opportunity to make ________.
3. das ist wohl möglich / das mag sein > that's ________ possible
4. Ich höre zu. > I am ______________.
5. Ich verstehe nicht. > I do not ________________.
6. Rechts fahren! / halten! > _______ to the right!
7. Meine Windschutzscheibe ist kaputt. > My __________ is broken.
8. Die Prüfung war hart. > The _________________ was tough.
9. Sie ist deswegen so aufgebracht / verärgert. > She is so ______ about this matter.
10. Wie lautet Ihre Anschrift hier in der Stadt? > What is your address in this _______?
11. Hiermit bestätige ich den Eingang Ihrer Lieferung. > I acknowledge ___________ of your delivery.
12. bitter schmecken > to ________ bitter
13. am Anfang > in the _______________
14. Wo ist der nächste Abschleppdienst? > Where is the ______ towing service?
15. Können Sie mich mit dieser Nummer verbinden? > _____ you connect me to this number?
16. Folgen Sie der Straßenbahnlinie. > __________ the tram lines.
17. Er hat sie für den Job empfohlen. > He __________________ her for the job.
18. Stell das Radio ab! > _______ off the radio!
19. auf einen Baum klettern > to climb up a _______

## TEST 5 Finden Sie die logische Entsprechung.

Arabic baker Bulgaria captain ~~church~~ continent death dwarf earth eat forbid French future listen milk mouth ocean restaurant river south

1. actor : theatre = priest : church
2. aeroplane : pilot = ship : ______
3. air : to breathe = food : to ______
4. Alps : mountain range = Nile : ______
5. yes : no = to allow : to ______
6. Ankara : Turkey = Sofia : ______
7. Arctic : north = Antarctic : ______
8. Astronomy : space = Geology : ______
9. Rhine : river = Atlantic : ______
10. Australia : English = Egypt : ______
11. Germany : German = France : ______
12. hair salon : hair dresser = bakery : ______
13. bee : honey = cow : ______
14. beginning : end = birth : ______
15. behind : front = past : ______
16. Belgium : country = Europe : ______
17. Bible : church = menu : ______
18. big : small = giant : ______
19. bird : beak = human : ______
20. book : to read = music : to ______

Finden Sie waagerecht oder senkrecht 11 Farben.

## TEST 6

| | | | | | | | | |
|---|---|---|---|---|---|---|---|---|
| **g** | **r** | **e** | **e** | **n** | w | b | d | a |
| e | b | r | o | w | n | l | k | w |
| n | p | i | n | k | u | u | j | h |
| r | p | u | r | p | l | e | o | i |
| u | g | c | a | b | m | v | r | t |
| g | y | e | l | l | o | w | a | e |
| r | j | w | m | a | l | r | n | e |
| e | z | g | l | c | w | e | g | i |
| y | s | b | u | k | c | d | e | c |

## TEST 7 Setzen Sie ein.

anything by cracked educated else equals fault head headache mistake cinema play right ~~scenery~~ speaks Sunday times to touch yesterday

1. fantastische Landschaft > fantastic scenery
2. ich kann nicht anders als > I can't do ______________ other than
3. sechs durch zwei ist drei > six divided by two __________ three
4. der Kopf tut mir weh > I've got a _________
5. geschieht ihm recht > serves him _________
6. letzten Sonntag > last __________
7. die Scheibe ist gesprungen > the pane is ____________
8. niemand anders / niemand sonst / weiter niemand > nobody _______
9. ein gebildeter Mensch > an ______________ man
10. eine Rolle spielen > to _______ a part / to act a part
11. einen Fehler machen > to make a ____________
12. mit dem Zug / mit der Bahn > ____ rail
13. im Kino > at the __________
14. in Verbindung stehen mit > to be in _______ with
15. ins Schwarze treffen > to hit the nail on the _______
16. er kann mehrere Sprachen > he __________ several languages
17. drei mal drei ist neun > three _________ three is nine
18. erst gestern > only ________________
19. es ist meine Schuld > it is my _________
20. es wird sicher regnen > it's sure ____ rain

## Was passt links und rechts zusammen?



| | |
|---|---|
| **1.** wall | finger |
| **2.** hand | tennis ball |
| **3.** racket | bulb |
| **4.** lamp | peel |
| **5.** banana | brick |
| | |
| **a.** suit | goal |
| **b.** computer | sugar |
| **c.** football | tie |
| **d.** book | mouse |
| **e.** coffee | page |
| | |
| **I.** Berlin | cork |
| **II.** weather | beer |
| **III.** night | darkness |
| **IV.** thirst | city |
| **V.** bottle | snow |
| | |
| **A.** tree | slice |
| **B.** television | trunk |
| **C.** bread | rules |
| **D.** leg | programme |
| **E.** grammar | foot |

## TEST 9 Welches Wort passt nicht in die Reihe?

1. blue brown ~~hard~~ yellow
2. sun star cloud moon
3. resentful jealous envious happy
4. apples beans broccoli peas
5. Albania Belgium Benelux Bulgaria
6. apple-juice beer service coffee
7. pineapple spinach apricots pears
8. eyebrows moustache beard throat
9. August weather October November
10. bathroom kitchen street bedroom
11. badminton tree billiards boxing
12. farmer fisherman hunter architect
13. bananas strawberries petrol blueberries
14. Berlin Zurich Hamburg Munich
15. hill picture vase bookshelf
16. visit scream sing laugh
17. lightning thunder handwriting storm
18. Chile Brazil Argentina Uruguay
19. brush cream fork comb
20. computer belt glove shirt

**Setzen Sie ein.**



accept ~~accident~~ as beer collect do dog electrician enquiry floor French if later laughing mountain tooth varies water what will

1. Haben Sie den Unfall gesehen? > Did you see the accident ____________?
2. Lachst du oder weinst du? > Are you ____________ or crying?
3. der höchste Berg der Welt > the highest ____________ in the world
4. Schluss damit! > That will ____!
5. wenn ich mich nicht irre > ____ I'm not mistaken
6. Der Elektriker hat unseren Fernseher repariert. > The ____________ repaired our television.
7. Bezahlen Sie jetzt oder später? > Would you like to pay now or ________?
8. sich einen Zahn ziehen lassen > to have a ________ pulled out
9. Die Temperatur ändert sich von Ort zu Ort. > The temperature ________ from place to place.
10. Sie müssen warten. > You _______ have to wait.
11. Nehmen Sie Kreditkarten an? > Do you ________ credit cards?
12. Im unteren Stock. > On the ________ below.
13. Um welche Zeit? / Um wieviel Uhr? > At _______ time?
14. Möchten Sie ein großes oder kleines Bier? > Do you want a large or small _______?
15. voll Wasser > filled with ________
16. soviel wie möglich > ____ much as possible
17. Er machte die russisch-französische Übersetzung. > He did the Russian to __________ translation.
18. Briefmarken sammeln > to ____________ stamps
19. Für Ihre Anfrage bedanken wir uns. > We thank you for your ____________.
20. Hunde an der Leine führen! > Keep your _____ on the leash!

## TEST 11 Was passt zusammen? Bilden Sie Sprichwörter oder Redensarten.

| | |
|---|---|
| **1.** A barking dog | **a)** come to an end. |
| **2.** A bird in the hand | **b)** even when he speaks the truth. |
| **3.** A friend in need | **c)** in love and war. |
| **4.** A liar is not believed | **d)** is a friend indeed. |
| **5.** A single stroke | **e)** is not gold. |
| **6.** Actions speak | **f)** is worth two in the bush. |
| **7.** All's fair | **g)** lead to Rome. |
| **8.** All roads | **h)** louder than words. |
| **9.** All that glitters | **i)** never bites. |
| **10.** All things must | **j)** won't fell an oak. |

| | |
|---|---|
| **11.** All's well | **a)** a tooth for a tooth. |
| **12.** An eye for an eye, | **b)** is his castle. |
| **13.** A man's home | **c)** little fish. |
| **14.** You've made your bed, | **d)** now lie in it. |
| **15.** Better late | **e)** tell no tales. |
| **16.** Big fish eat | **f)** than never. |
| **17.** Brevity is | **g)** that ends well. |
| **18.** Caution is | **h)** the mother of wisdom. |
| **19.** Cold hands, | **i)** the soul of wit. |
| **20.** Dead men | **j)** warm heart |

**Setzen Sie ein.** 



benefit dishes down enter late love obliged only post read receipt second smoke ~~spend~~ succeeded such thinking this wake wine

1. das Wochenende verbringen > to spend the weekend
2. ich bin Ihnen sehr verbunden > I am greatly ____________ to you
3. ich koste den Wein > I'll taste the _______
4. Wecken Sie mich bitte um ... > Please _______ me at ...
5. den Brief einwerfen > to __________ the letter
6. der / die / das Zweite > the __________
7. das Geschirr spülen > to do the _______
8. die Zeitung lesen > to _______ the paper
9. ein Gespräch beginnen > to ________ into conversation
10. ein solcher Mensch / solch ein Mensch > _______ a person
11. eine Zigarette rauchen > to ________ a cigarette
12. einen Vorteil haben von > to ____________ from
13. Wir haben Ihre Reklamation erhalten. > We confirm ____________ of your complaint.
14. im Laufe dieser Woche > in the course of _______ week
15. an die Arbeit gehen / sich ans Werk machen > to get _______ to work
16. Woran denkst du? > What are you ______________ about?
17. erst heute > _______ today
18. es ist mir gelungen > I have ________________
19. es wird spät > it's getting _______
20. aus Liebe heiraten > to marry for _______

## TEST 13 Kreuzworträtsel

### WAAGERECHT

1 Can you s**** fluent French?

4 The s******** carried many passengers down the Mississippi.

9 The child is crying because its t** is broken.

10 He has a mobile p****, but I don't know the number.

11 The doctor gave me some ear drops for my e******.

14 He can't s** without his spectacles.

15 We baked her a c*** for her birthday.

16 He's a s******* here, nobody knows him.

19 The child wants i** mother.

21 Wipe your hands on the n***** next to your plate.

23 That t*** has no leaves in the winter.

26 N*, he is not here.

27 E** is a popular seafood in this area.

29 I a* your new boss.

30 The orphanage g*** money from charitable people.

32 Hello! Is a***** home?

33 There a** many good pubs here.

35 I need some lemons and sugar to make l*******.

36 He bought a k*** of potatoes.

38 He's wearing a bow t** to the party.

39 She needs some driving l******, will you teach her?

42 Belfast is an I**** city.

43 I need some fresh a**, open the windows.

45 I need to smoke, I need a c********.

46 Go to sleep, you have to wake up e**** tomorrow.

**SENKRECHT**

1 Oregano is a good s******** in a salad.

2 He e****** to get the job without any difficulties.

3 I can hear someone k******* on the door.

4 She made a meat and vegetable s*** for supper.

5 Please give this t* him.

6 She uses a lot of e** shadow on her eyelids.

7 Her b** is visible through her white dress.

8 The children hugged t**** parents.

12 Have you r*** this book?

13 He hates cigarettes, but he smokes one c**** a day.

17 I had this suit made by a t***** in town.

18 She o***** the door and let them in.

20 He hurt his t** when his foot hit the door.

22 I can't find the k** to this lock.

24 He whispered in her e**.

25 This is an e********, please call the police!

**28** Did the doctor prescribe any m******* for your pain?

**31** How many t**** have you visited this museum?

**33** This shirt is dirty, could I have a****** one?

**34** They moved i*** their new house.

**35** The colour l**** reminds me of lavender.

**37** You t*** very easily, you have no stamina.

**40** The sailor is away at s**.

**41** She s** at the desk next to me when I was in school.

**44** I* is very cold today.

Welches Lösungswort ergibt sich in der senkrechten Reihe?

| | | | | | | | | | | | |
|---|---|---|---|---|---|---|---|---|---|---|---|
| | | R | H | | N | | C | | R | | S |
| | | G | | R | | F | F | | | | |
| | | | P | | N | G | | | N | | |
| | L | | P | H | | N | T | | | | |
| | | F | | X | | | | | | | |
| L | | | P | | R | D | | | | | |
| | | W | | L | F | | | | | | |
| | | | T | | G | | R | | | | |
| | B | | | R | | | | | | | |
| | C | | M | | L | | | | | | |
| | | T | | R | T | L | | | | | |
| | | | S | N | | K | | | | | |

## TEST 15 Setzen Sie die Buchstaben in die richtige Reihenfolge, um die logische Entsprechung zu finden.

1. bookstore : books = optician : [ssaselg] glasses
2. boxing : gloves = tennis : [takrce] ____________
3. brave : afraid = bravery : [reaf] ____________
4. Brazil : Brazilians = Mexico : [easixMcn] ____________
5. Brussels : Belgium = Athens : [ereceG] ____________
6. Buddha : Buddhism = Christ : [yiahtitsiCrn] ____________
7. building : storeys = apartment : [omors] ____________
8. bus : bus stop = train : train [tastoni] ____________
9. campsite : hotel = cheap : [vexsnieep] ____________
10. car : horn = bicycle : [lelb] ____________
11. sleigh : horses = car : [neigen] ____________
12. car : wheel = table : [elg] ____________
13. lamp : ceiling = carpet : [oorlf] ____________
14. cheap : expensive = canteen : [attuerrnas] ____________
15. cheetah : fast = snail : [lwso] ____________
16. chocolate : bar = truffles : [obx] ____________
17. Christianity : Bible = Islam : [aornK] ____________
18. church : to pray = school : to [dtsyu] ____________
19. cigarettes : lungs = alcohol : [ierlv] ____________
20. cigarettes : vegetables = sick : [elhthya] ____________

**Setzen Sie ein.**



age been books change cut Catholic fastest finish Leave meat morning never only people placed running ~~so~~ stay used vegetables

1. ja, ich denke schon > yes, I think _so_
2. Haben Sie gekochtes Gemüse? > Have you got any cooked __________?
3. man kann nie wissen > you __________ know
4. über Nacht bleiben / übernachten > to __________ overnight
5. Ich fahre morgen sehr früh ab. > I am leaving early tomorrow __________.
6. Ich möchte Braten mit Kartoffeln. > I would like some __________ with potatoes.
7. Geh aus dem Zimmer, damit ich Ruhe habe. > __________ the room so that I can have some peace.
8. sehr viele Leute > a great many __________
9. Der Rest ist für Sie. / Stimmt so. > Keep the __________.
10. sich in den Finger schneiden > to __________ one's finger
11. Dieser Athlet läuft am schnellsten. > This athlete runs the __________.
12. wir sind gleich alt > we are the same __________
13. Sind Sie Katholik oder Protestant? > Are you __________ or Protestant?
14. mit fließendem Wasser > with __________ water
15. Am ... habe ich bei Ihnen eine Bestellung aufgegeben. > On ... I __________ an order with you.
16. wir waren früher gute Freunde > we __________ to be good friends
17. von Anfang bis Ende > from start to __________
18. Es gab einen Unfall. > There has __________ an accident.
19. Bücher aus zweiter Hand > second-hand __________
20. nur noch 3 Minuten > __________ 3 minutes left

## TEST 17 Was passt zusammen? Bilden Sie Sprichwörter oder Redensarten.

| | | | |
|---|---|---|---|
| 1. | Do not throw pearls | a) | before they hatch. |
| 2. | Don't count your chickens | b) | before swine. |
| 3. | Easy come, | c) | easy go. |
| 4. | Faith will | d) | first served. |
| 5. | First come, | e) | flies than vinegar. |
| 6. | Fish and wine | f) | go together. |
| 7. | Four eyes see | g) | laughs longest. |
| 8. | God helps those | h) | more than two. |
| 9. | He who laughs last, | i) | move mountains. |
| 10. | Honey catches more | j) | who help themselves. |

| | | | |
|---|---|---|---|
| 11. | Honour to whom | a) | but great ones escape. |
| 12. | If you grease well, | b) | God disposes. |
| 13. | In the country of the blind, | c) | honour is due. |
| 14. | It is better to give | d) | is blind. |
| 15. | Knowledge | e) | is power. |
| 16. | Lies have | f) | short legs. |
| 17. | Little thieves are hanged, | g) | than to receive. |
| 18. | Love | h) | the one-eyed man is king. |
| 19. | Lucky at cards, | i) | unlucky in love. |
| 20. | Man proposes, | j) | you speed well. |

**Setzen Sie die Buchstaben in die richtige Reihenfolge, um die logische Entsprechung zu finden.**

1. present : packaging = letter : [oeenvelp] envelope
2. pudding : eat = air : [haretbe] ______________
3. pullover : wool = belt : [eetrlha] ______________
4. rain : wet = towel : [ryd] ______________
5. Rhine : Germany = Nile : [gptyE] ______________
6. rich : poor = millionaire : [ergbga] ______________
7. ring : gold = tyre : [rbuerb] ______________
8. robber : rob = thief : [atles] ______________
9. rocks : pebbles = water : [rposd] ______________
10. Rome : Italy = Vienna : [iutaAsr] ______________
11. room : chairs = bus : [etsas] ______________
12. rose : flower = nightingale : [dibr] ______________
13. Russia : Russian = France : [hnrFec] ______________
14. safety : danger = safe : [urgaodesn] ______________
15. sandals : sunshine = Wellington boots : [anir] ______________
16. Easter rabbit : Easter = Santa Claus : [hCirtsasm] ______________
17. sausage : butcher = bread : [earkb ] ______________
18. wrong : right = lie : [trhtu] ______________
19. script : alphabets = music : [oents] ______________
20. sea : coast = picture : [mrfea] ______________

## TEST 19 Setzen Sie ein.

car children ~~comfort~~ electricity exchange feel fits learn lose Look milk name pass profession sign Sit table than today trust

1. das ist kein Trost für mich > that's no comfort to me
2. den Verstand verlieren > to _______ one's mind
3. Vertrauen haben zu > to have confidence in / to _________
4. Setzen Sie sich! > _____ down!
5. die Milch ist sauer > the _______ has spoilt
6. Wie hoch ist der Wechselkurs? > What is the ______________ rate?
7. Sieh mich an! > _______ at me!
8. dieser Anzug sitzt gut > this suit _______ well
9. ein Zeichen geben > to make a _______
10. eine Prüfung bestehen > to _______ an examination
11. einen Beruf ausüben > to practise a _________________
12. Wir müssen Strom sparen. > We must conserve ___________________.
13. alle Kinder > all the ______________
14. Notieren Sie Ihren Namen und Ihre Adresse. > Write down your _______ and address.
15. er ist zwanzig Jahre jünger als ich > he is twenty years younger _______ me
16. heute ist Donnerstag > _________ is Thursday
17. Ist der Wagen versichert? > Is the _____ insured?
18. auf den Tisch stellen > to put on the _________
19. Lust haben zu > to _________ like
20. auswendig lernen > to _________ by heart

## Was passt links und rechts zusammen?

| | | |
|---|---|---|
| 1. | chin | pope |
| 2. | church | thunder |
| 3. | lightning | glass |
| 4. | wine | petrol |
| 5. | car | beard |

| | | |
|---|---|---|
| a. | shirt | cloud |
| b. | sports | letters |
| c. | sky | collar |
| d. | music | notes |
| e. | word | Olympics |

| | | |
|---|---|---|
| I. | tree | answer |
| II. | face | verdict |
| III. | question | nose |
| IV. | judge | wood |
| V. | cause | effect |

| | | |
|---|---|---|
| A. | heater | rent |
| B. | plant | elections |
| C. | money | wallet |
| D. | apartment | warmth |
| E. | parties | leaf |

**TEST 21** Finden Sie waagerecht oder senkrecht 24 Körperteile.

| | | | | | | | | | | | | |
|---|---|---|---|---|---|---|---|---|---|---|---|---|
| z | b | d | c | e | h | n | t | s | s | m | h | h |
| e | e | c | t | y | c | q | h | h | t | o | b | a |
| c | a | h | h | e | a | x | u | o | o | u | o | n |
| h | r | i | r | b | b | t | m | u | m | t | s | d |
| e | d | n | o | r | t | f | b | l | a | h | o | s |
| e | b | f | a | o | z | z | h | d | c | b | m | h |
| k | r | f | t | w | b | o | n | e | h | f | m | j |
| p | e | a | **f** | **i** | **n** | **g** | **e** | **r** | **n** | **a** | **i** | **l** |
| p | a | c | o | z | t | o | n | g | u | e | t | d |
| x | s | e | n | o | s | e | e | s | h | s | o | x |
| e | t | f | i | n | g | e | r | k | s | r | o | q |
| w | p | n | e | c | k | h | a | i | r | s | t | l |
| m | h | h | e | a | d | p | k | n | e | e | h | l |

**Setzen Sie ein.**

about about care glad hand ~~here~~ home less long manners morning or please radio tell turn voice were whenever yesterday

1. Darf ich hier parken? > Can I park here ?
2. über kurz oder lang / früher oder später > sooner ____ later
3. ich bin an der Reihe / ich bin dran > it's my _______
4. das ist mir egal > I don't _______
5. jedesmal, wenn > _______________
6. mehr oder weniger > more or _______
7. es gehört sich nicht > it is bad ________
8. gestern morgen > _________________ morning
9. offen gestanden > to _______ the truth
10. sich sorgen um > to be uneasy / to worry _________
11. Die Badezimmer waren unhygienisch. > The bathrooms _______ not clean.
12. mit leiser Stimme > in a low _________
13. Bitte einen Tisch für 2 Personen. > A table for two, ___________.
14. im Radio hören > to hear on the _________
15. in der Hand halten > to hold in one's _______
16. von früh bis spät > from _____________ till night
17. es ist mir lieb, dass > I am _______ that
18. etwa zehn Jahre > _________ 10 years
19. zu Hause sein > to be at _______
20. Auf Wiedersehen! / Bis bald! > Good-bye! / So _______! / See you (again)!

## TEST 23 Setzen Sie die Buchstaben in die richtige Reihenfolge, um die gegenteilige Bedeutung zu finden.

1. to give - to [aekt] take
2. to accept - to [ueefrs] ____________
3. to freeze - to [teml] ____________
4. to push - to [lulp] ____________
5. to approve - to [eoipapsvrd] ____________
6. to lock - to [onklcu] ____________
7. to succeed - to [alfi] ____________
8. to appear - to [aaiprdpse] ____________
9. to lend - to [rworob] ____________
10. to ascend - to [ncedsde] ____________
11. to search - to [dinf] ____________
12. to trust - to [iuttrssd] ____________
13. to break - to [ifx] ____________
14. to halve - to [beolud] ____________
15. to forget - to [berermme] ____________
16. to agree - to [reiasdge] ____________
17. to tie - to [inteu] ____________
18. to behave - to [hvibsemea] ____________
19. to throw - to [tachc] ____________
20. to follow - to [dela] ____________

**Setzen Sie europäische Länder ein.**
**Welches Land ergibt sich in der senkrechten Reihe? (The …)**

| | | | | | | | | | | | | | | | | |
|---|---|---|---|---|---|---|---|---|---|---|---|---|---|---|---|---|
| | | | | | | S | P | | | | | | | | | |
| | | | | | | | | S | W | | D | | N | | | |
| | | | | | | | | | | | | R | K | | | |
| | | | | | | | | | | | | N | G | | R | |
| | | | | | | S | L | | V | | N | | | | | |
| | | | | | | | | | | | | S | S | | | |
| | | | | | | | | | S | | | V | | K | | |
| | | | | P | | R | T | | G | | L | | | | | |
| | | | | | | R | | M | | | | | | | | |
| S | W | | T | Z | | R | L | | N | | | | | | | |
| | | | | | | | | G | | | L | | V | | | |

## TEST 25 Setzen Sie ein.

case cook day glasses hands history matter May ~~plastic~~ raining razor run sharp slow stroke Summer taste temperature thing Where

1. Kann ich eine Plastiktüte haben? > May I have a plastic bag?
2. das Essen kochen > to ________ / to prepare the meal
3. Was für ein Glück! > What a ___________ of luck!
4. das schadet nichts > that does not ___________
5. Hat man je so was gesehen? > Did you ever see such a ________?
6. Ich habe meine Brille zerbrochen. > I have broken my ____________.
7. Ich möchte mir die Hände waschen. > I want to wash my _________.
8. Mein Wagen hat kein Benzin mehr. > My car has ____ out of gas.
9. Der Sommer ist vorbei. > ___________ is over.
10. Geschichte studieren > to study _____________
11. die Uhr geht fünf Minuten nach > the clock is five minutes _____
12. Sie hatte hohe Temperatur / hohes Fieber. > She had a high _________.
13. Wie schmeckt's? > How does it _________?
14. am Tag vorher / tags zuvor > the ______ before
15. Wo ist die nächste Werkstatt? > _________ is the next repair service / garage?
16. Es regnete, deshalb konnten wir nicht rausgehen. > It was ___________ so we couldn't go out.
17. Steckdose für den Rasierapparat > socket for the _______
18. Dürfen wir ein Feuer anmachen? > ______ we light a fire?
19. auf jeden Fall > in any ________ / at any rate
20. Punkt 5 Uhr > at 5 o'clock _________

**Finden Sie die logische Entsprechung.** **TEST 26**

conductor cutlery darkness dead glass glass hard heater Indonesia peace person police red referee roar ~~stage~~ temperature uniform white write

1. cinema : screen = theatre : stage
2. class : teacher = orchestra : ____________________
3. hospital : ill = graveyard : ____________________
4. clock : time = thermometer : ____________________
5. clown : costume = soldier : ____________________
6. cock : to crow = lion : to ____________________
7. oil : black = milk : ____________________
8. coffee : cup = wine : ____________________
9. cold : air conditioner = warm : ____________________
10. composer : to compose = author : to ____________________
11. court : judge = football game : ____________________
12. fire : fire brigade = crime : ____________________
13. cucumber : green = tomato : ____________________
14. cup : crockery = fork : ____________________
15. cupboard : wood = window pane : ____________________
16. cushion : soft = concrete : ____________________
17. damage : car = wound : ____________________
18. danger : safety = war : ____________________
19. day : light = night : ____________________
20. Delhi : India = Jakarta : ____________________

## TEST 27 Kreuzworträtsel

### WAAGERECHT

1 He p****** the fence a bright red.

6 I t**** to call you, but you weren't home.

8 They made him a tempting o****.

9 We manufacture these products in our own f*******.

11 He's d******* and isn't allowed to eat sweets.

12 The a***** patient was breathless and needed oxygen.

14 The s*** will dock tomorrow.

15 The Last S***** is a famous painting.

17 He drove a** the way.

19 Keep a stiff upper l**!

20 The driver of the v** was friendly.

21 Tell me as soon as he e***** the office.

22 The pubs b*** their own beer.

24 My niece and n***** are visiting me.

26 Did you like the sound of the b******* in Scotland?

29 Don't brush your hair with that dirty h********.

30 Please l**** me alone!

31 Please e**** all the data in the computer.

32 I want icecream for d******

**SENKRECHT**

1 She's as p**** as a peacock.

2 The prices have gone up due to i********.

3 They ate t***** at Thanksgiving dinner.

4 He had no d********* in solving the puzzle.

5 The d*** of the ship was crowded.

6 He looks good in those t*******.

7 Very few I**** still speak Gaelic.

10 Don't s****** without chewing your food.

13 She a********* me with a request.

14 I'm in s****** heaven when I eat chocolate.

16 He loves apple p** with ice cream.

17 Look at that a******** flying high in the air!

18 I can't r******* his name.

23 This pie is made with a*****.

25 I can't read the small p**** in this book.

27 He whispered s**** nothings in her ear.

28 She talks too m***.

## TEST 28 Setzen Sie ein.

better do drive enough hardly health not quarter ~~reason~~ rule there times tomorrow touch turn walk well with would younger

1. eben deswegen > for that very reason
2. ich bin es leid / ich habe genug davon > I have had ________ of it
3. ich möchte lieber > I __________ rather
4. rechts fahren > to __________ on the right
5. mein jüngerer Bruder > my ______________ brother
6. seine Schularbeiten / Hausaufgaben machen > to ____ one's homework
7. jemandem böse sein > to be angry ________ someone
8. gesund sein > to be in good ____________
9. sich wohl fühlen > to be ________
10. ein paarmal > several __________
11. eine Viertelstunde > a ______________ of an hour
12. einen Spaziergang machen > to go for a ________
13. sie macht kaum Fehler > she __________ makes any mistakes
14. um die Ecke biegen > to ________ the corner
15. in der Regel > as a ________
16. von sich hören lassen > to keep in ________
17. morgen früh > ________________ morning
18. erst morgen > ______ until tomorrow
19. es ist nicht nötig > __________ is no need
20. etwas Besseres > something ____________

## Welches Wort passt in die logische Reihe?



1. spring, summer, _________, winter
2. May, June, _________, August
3. one, three, five, ___________
4. __________, Friday, Saturday, Sunday
5. the sun, the moon and the __________
6. January, _________, March, April
7. two, ________, six, eight
8. right, left, forward, ____________
9. Monday, Tuesday, __________, Thursday
10. first, second, _________, fourth
11. yesterday, ________, tomorrow, the day after tomorrow
12. always, often, seldom, _________
13. North, __________, East, West
14. past, present, ______________
15. in front, at the back / rear, __________, below

## TEST 30 Kreuzworträtsel

**WAAGERECHT**

1 She broke the tea c**.

3 I gave a b**** summary of what happened.

6 He is a famous a**** at the national theatre.

9 The river R**** flows through Europe.

10 A car is the only means of t******** here.

13 This book is from the b******* near my house.

14 That's the p***** who married them.

17 Does the timing s*** you?

18 We're visiting the national m***** today.

20 She doesn't look her a**.

22 She c** swim very fast.

23 He had e** and rolls for breakfast.

24 She's so p*****, she doesn't need make-up.

25 She's isn't a*** to come.

27 P***** borders on Germany.

29 You'll need an u******* if it rains.

31 I have an i******** meeting this morning.

34 The office is on the n**** floor.

36 He bought himself a Swiss army k****.

37 There are policemen at e**** corner.

38 He's pierced his left e**.

**SENKRECHT**

1 My c** is in the garage.

2 She is suffering from food p********.

3 She has cancer in her right b*****.

4 I was i********* to my new colleagues.

5 My f*** has 3 rooms.

7 Wear a c** if you're playing in the sun.

8 We left o** house early.

11 S***** is my favourite seafood.

12 You o** me a lot of money.

15 Don't keep running here and t****!

16 She's one c********* taller than me.

17 The baby was tired and went to s****.

19 He s** on his mother's lap.

20 We need an a******** to take him to hospital.

21 I need a bottle o***** to open the bottles.

26 He drank a glass of b***** to help his cold.

28 She bit her l** in agitation.

30 H*** you heard the news?

32 M** aren't as perceptive as women.

33 Switch o** the music!

35 She knows h** own weaknesses.

## TEST 31 Setzen Sie ein.

car charge coming damage dog door drink God Good hospital machine Make Noon No performance ~~salt~~ sea shoes surprise too

1. Das Salz kommt aus dem Toten Meer. > This salt comes from the Dead Sea.
2. Fasse dich kurz! > _______ it short!
3. Ich komme gleich! > I'm just __________!
4. Schaden anrichten > to do harm / to cause __________
5. Beginn der Vorstellung um ... > The _______________ begins at ...
6. Wein trinken > to ________ wine
7. Ihr Wagen behindert den Verkehr. > Your _____ is holding up the traffic.
8. Die Maschine verbraucht zuviel Strom. > This ____________ uses too much electricity.
9. Sie müssen ins Krankenhaus. > You must go to the _____________.
10. Hiermit stellen wir Ihnen folgende Beträge in Rechnung ... > We herewith _______ you the following ...
11. Einfahrt verboten! > ___ entry!
12. übers Meer segeln > to sail across the _____
13. Mittag ist die heißeste Tageszeit. > _______ is the hottest part of the day.
14. Bitte putzen Sie meine Schuhe. > Please clean my ________.
15. Um Himmels willen! > _______ heavens!
16. an die Tür klopfen > to knock at the _______
17. Der Hund bellt. > The _____ is barking.
18. Gott sei Dank! > Thank _____! / Fortunately!
19. zu meiner Überraschung > to my ______________
20. Würden Sie auch den Ölstand nachprüfen? > Could you check the oil, _____?

## Finden Sie die logische Entsprechung.



beautiful boss ~~crocodile~~ day deep drink Dutch fleet fork head hiss lie oil reap round shampoo summer twelve verse water

1. sea : shark = river : crocodile
2. second : minute = hour : ____________
3. fish : school = ship : ____________
4. shoe : foot = hat : ____________
5. six : three = twenty four : ____________
6. skin : soap = hair : ____________
7. skyscraper : tall = well : ____________
8. lion : to roar = snake : to ____________
9. snow : winter = sunshine : ____________
10. sofa : to sit = bed : to ____________
11. soldier : general = secretary : ____________
12. solid : liquid = ice : ____________
13. poem : stanza = song : ____________
14. soup : spoon = cake : ____________
15. South Africa : diamonds = Saudi Arabia : ____________
16. Spain : Spanish = Holland : ____________
17. spider : ugly = butterfly : ____________
18. plate : to eat = glass : to ____________
19. spring : to sow = autumn : to ____________
20. square : angular = circle : ____________

**TEST 33** **Setzen Sie die fehlenden Vokale „a“, „e“, „o“ ein, um den Witz zu verstehen.**

A man has _ s_us_g_ st_nd dir_ctly _pp_sit_ _ b_nk.

_n _ld fri_nd c_m_s _nd _sks him:

„C_n y_u l_nd m_ s_m_ m_n_y?“

„I'm s_rry, I c_n't!“

„_nd why n_t?“

„B_c_us_ I h_v_ _ c_ntr_ct with th_ b_nk!“

„Wh_t kind _f _ c_ntr_ct?“

„I d_n't l_nd _ny m_n_y _nd th_y d_n't s_ll _ny s_us_g_s!“

**Setzen Sie ein.**



advance age back bread carry coat cross fact going mistake need nowhere people question same something something ~~south~~ until watch

1. ich fahre nach Süden > I'm travelling south
2. das führt zu nichts > that leads ____________
3. ich bin gleich wieder da > I'll be _______ shortly / in a bit
4. ich muss weggehen > I must be off / I must be _________
5. meine Uhr geht vor > my _________ is fast
6. etwas stimmt nicht > ______________ is wrong
7. den Mantel anziehen > to put on one's _______
8. die Grenze überschreiten > to _________ the border / frontier
9. die meisten Leute > most __________
10. ein Stück Brot > a piece of _________
11. eine Frage stellen > to ask a ______________
12. eine schwere Last tragen > to _________ a heavy load
13. wir sind gleich alt > we are the _______ age
14. im Voraus > in ____________
15. in der Tat > in ________
16. er ist in meinem Alter > he is my _____
17. erst morgen > not _________ tomorrow
18. es ist nicht nötig > there is no _______
19. etwas Gutes > ________________ good
20. aus Versehen > by ____________

## TEST 35 Setzen Sie die Buchstaben in die richtige Reihenfolge, um die logische Entsprechung zu finden.

1. Germany : German = Denmark : [iahnsD] Danish
2. desert : sand = sea : [eawrt] ______________
3. dog : animal = flower : [lnpta] ______________
4. dog : to bark = cat : [to emw] ______________
5. eagle : to fly = whale : [to mwis] ______________
6. early : late = breakfast : [rniden] ______________
7. elephant : big = mouse : [lmlsa] ______________
8. elephant : trunk = human : [oesn] ______________
9. child : pocket money = employee : [aayslr] ______________
10. England : monarchy = France : [lecubirp] ______________
11. evening : time of the day = autumn : [nseosa] ______________
12. expressionism : painting = baroque : [hcureterícta] ______________
13. eye : blind = ear : [efad] ______________
14. eye : to see = ear : [to erah] ______________
15. fan : heat = heating : [odlc] ______________
16. far : near = distance : [reesansn] ______________
17. to gain weight : to lose weight = fat : [hnti] ______________
18. father : daughter = king : [renscisp] ______________

**Setzen Sie die Buchstaben in die richtige Reihenfolge, um die gegenteilige Bedeutung zu finden.**



1. direct - [neitircd] indirect
2. perfect - [fmcerepti] ____________________
3. loose - [higtt] ____________________
4. together - [eaeaprst] ____________________
5. yesterday - [wrooromt] ____________________
6. flexible - [bxelniflie] ____________________
7. liquid - [oidls] ____________________
8. now - [eatrl] ____________________
9. offensive - [eesvindfe] ____________________
10. noisy - [eutqi] ____________________
11. scarce - [tnbaduan] ____________________
12. arid - [telfrei] ____________________
13. tolerant - [ateonlinrt] ____________________
14. spicy - [lndba] ____________________
15. arrogant - [uebhml] ____________________
16. plausible - [iulmliepasb] ____________________
17. shortsighted - [hgeiotslngd] ____________________
18. strong - [kewa] ____________________

## TEST 37 Setzen Sie ein.

another ago ~~any~~ back coffee great hundreds meet nationality over page park parking road seriously skidded Take That would Welcome

1. Haben Sie Zigaretten? > Have you got _any_ cigarettes?
2. Das ist ja großartig! > It's simply _________!
3. Lassen Sie sich Zeit! > _______ your time!
4. Ich möchte ein Einzelzimmer mit Dusche. > I _________ like a single room with a shower.
5. Seien Sie willkommen! > _____________!
6. seinen Wagen parken > to _______ one's car
7. Möchten Sie noch eine Tasse Tee? > Would you like _________ cup of tea?
8. Die Sache ist erledigt! > _______ settles the matter!
9. Ihr Auto rutschte auf der vereisten Straße. > Her car _________ on the icy road.
10. Wann werden wir uns wieder treffen? > When shall we _______ again?
11. Niemand ist ernstlich verletzt. > Nobody is ______________ hurt.
12. Bitte wenden! > Please turn _______!
13. In dieser Straße gibt es Parkuhren. > There are ____________ meters in this street.
14. unten auf der Seite > at the bottom of the _______
15. vor einiger Zeit > some time _____
16. Er ist deutscher Nationalität. > His _______________ is German.
17. rückwärts fahren > to _______ up / to reverse
18. Führt diese Straße direkt in die Stadt? > Does this _______ lead straight into the city?
19. jemand zum Kaffee einladen > to invite someone for a cup of _____
20. Hunderte von > ______________ of

## Welche Körperteile sind gemeint?



1. to hug someone: arms ____________________
2. to chew food: ____________________
3. to think: ____________________
4. to kiss someone: ____________________
5. to hit someone hard: ____________________
6. to smell: ____________________
7. to see: ____________________
8. to hear: ____________________
9. to taste: ____________________
10. it beats: ____________________
11. to clap: ____________________
12. to point: ____________________
13. to feel: ____________________
14. you get it cut at the barber's: ____________________
15. you shave it: ____________________
16. you wear a necklace around it: ____________________
17. to breathe: ____________________
18. to show one's strength: ____________________
19. to tap it to music: ____________________
20. to run fast: ____________________

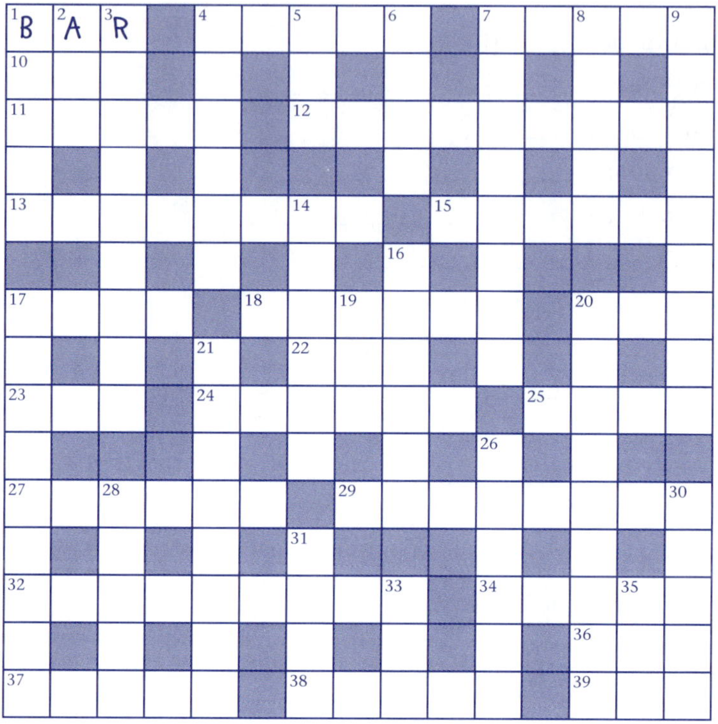


## WAAGERECHT

1 Let's have a drink at the b**.

4 Surfing is a s****.

7 This cycle didn't cost me much, it was c****.

10 He's very active despite his a**.

11 Have you tried the l**** beer?

12 Could you t******** this English document into French?

13 S******* the white clothes from the coloured ones.

15 I'd like a b***** of water, please

17 China is in A***.

18 Is a***** there?

20 The wine is in an old v**.

22 Can you g** me a coke?

23 Don't write with that p**.

24 My aunt's son is my c***** .

25 I love i*** soda.

27 Could you r***** my broken chair?

29 We bought pottery from the c******* shop.

32 I need a g******** to help me tour the city.

34 I'd like a glass of fresh g**** juice.

36 Do wear a t** for the interview!

37 The dessert is too s****.

38 Could I have a d**** to dry my hair?

39 The e** of the movie was disappointing.

SENKRECHT

1 He's juggling with multi-coloured b****.

2 I finished the work long a**.

3 Check in at the hotel r******** .

4 Your s***** will be raised this month.

5 Get o** of my house!

6 I want our t*** to win the match.

7 Be courteous to every c******* in the shop.

8 What is the e**** time of departure?

9 The rain p******** us from playing the match.

14 We're having ox t***** soup today.

16 I didn't see the n***** about the meeting.

17 He loves a******** soup.

19 Y**, I would like that.

20 Did you v******** her for polio?

21 The driver died in the a*******.

26 The boy is in d***** of drowning in the river.

28 She won the first p**** in the competition.

30 It's unsafe to drive at a high s**** in the rain.

31 She ate her f*** slowly.

33 Where is the car k**?

35 I need a hair p** for my hair.

## TEST 40 Setzen Sie ein.

aches ~~bad~~ coat else else funny height hungry nothing on ought Our pay rate rising side thirteen tomorrow understand weather

1. das ist nicht so schlimm > it's not as bad as all that
2. ich bin hungrig / ich habe Hunger > I'm ________
3. ich sollte eigentlich arbeiten > I ________ to work
4. bei schönem Wetter > when the ____________ is fine
5. der Kopf tut mir weh > my head ________
6. Verstehen Sie deutsch? > Do you _________________ German?
7. die Sonne geht auf > the sun is __________
8. Wie hoch ist der Wechselkurs? > What is the exchange _______?
9. ein komischer Einfall > a ________ idea
10. eine Strafe zahlen > to _____ a fine
11. einen Mantel tragen > to wear a _______
12. Wir sind 2 Erwachsene und 4 Kinder. > _____ party consists of 2 adults and 4 children.
13. wir sind gleich groß > we are the same ________
14. alles andere > everything _______
15. im zweiten Stock wohnen > to live ___ the second floor
16. dreizehn Meter lang > ______________ metres long
17. Ich fahre morgen ab > I'm leaving ______________
18. es ist nichts übriggeblieben > there is ____________ left
19. etwas anderes > something _______
20. auf der rechten Seite > on the right / on the right hand _______

**Setzen Sie das richtige Fragewort ein.** 

How How How How Since Till What What What What When Where Where Where Which ~~Who~~ Who Whom Whose Why

1. Who is that? - That is my boss.
2. ________ do you come from? - From Switzerland.
3. ________ do you live? - In Paris.
4. ________ does that cost? - Only a few dollars.
5. ________ are you calling up? - My parents.
6. ________ are you lending the book to? - To my friend.
7. ________ many children do you have? - A boy and a girl.
8. ________ wallet is that? - It is mine.
9. ________ actor do you like best? - Charlie Chaplin.
10. ________ often do you have class? - Twice a week.
11. ________ long does the journey take? - Six hours.
12. ________ much time do you have? - 3 hours.
13. ________ did you get married? - 10 years ago.
14. ________ aren't you going to school? - Because I'm ill.
15. ________ are you travelling to? - To Madrid
16. ________ are you thinking of? - Of my work.
17. ________ do you use the computer for? - For e-mail.
18. ________ are you waiting for? - For the bus.
19. ________ when have you lived abroad? - Since 1998.
20. ________ when will you be here? - Till Monday.

## TEST 42 Welches Wort passt nicht in die Reihe?

1. ~~sand~~ - sugar - salt - pepper
2. Denmark - Sweden - Finland - Greece
3. lid - cork - roof - match
4. to stand - to jump - to spring - to climb
5. television - curtains - heater - sky
6. cucumber - carrots - fish - potatoes
7. dolphin - shark - herring - tuna
8. German - Bavarian - Italian - Polish
9. December - summer - autumn - winter
10. fly - mosquito - goat - bee
11. floppy - monitor - printer - pencil
12. Europe - Austria - Switzerland - Poland
13. can opener - pot - corkscrew - bottle opener
14. friendly - dumb - stingy - intolerant
15. duck - spider - turkey - goose
16. figs - cherries - kiwis - tomatoes
17. window - book - wall - floor
18. finger - hand - thumb - face
19. grey - strong - green - purple
20. belt - trouser - hat - suspenders

**Setzen Sie ein.**

## TEST 43

by car corner ~~declare~~ excludes faithful give judge latest need night no other present sauna sick television try outdoors worry

1. Haben Sie etwas zu verzollen? > Do you have anything to declare?
2. nach der neuesten Mode > according to the __________ fashion
3. Ich gebe Ihnen eine Spritze. > I'm going to _______ you an injection.
4. Ich möchte einen Wagen mieten. > I would like to rent a _____.
5. schlafen gehen / zu Bett gehen > to retire for the _________ / to go to bed
6. Unsere Kinder spielen gern draußen. > Our children like to play ________.
7. jemandem treu bleiben > to remain ____________ to somebody
8. Der Elektriker hat unseren Fernseher repariert. > The electrician repaired our _________________.
9. Beurteile Menschen nicht nach dem Äußeren. > Don't ________ people by appearances.
10. sich Sorgen / Gedanken machen über > to ___________ about
11. Die Transportkosten sind nicht im Angebot enthalten. > The offer ______________ transportation costs.
12. sie lieben sich > they love each _________
13. mir ist schlecht / übel > I feel ill / I feel _______
14. in die Ecke stellen > to put in the ___________
15. unter keinen Umständen / auf gar keinen Fall > on ____ account
16. mit Gewalt > ______ force
17. Er wird sein Bestes versuchen. > He'll ____ his best.
18. Brauchen Sie ein Einzel- oder Doppelzimmer? > Do you _______ a single or a double room?
19. Ist eine Sauna vorhanden? > Do you have _________ facilities?
20. anwesend sein > to be ____________

## TEST 44 Finden Sie die logische Entsprechung.

believe close defence departure divide dog dry familiar finish head lazy ~~mayor~~ patient rocket sing sweet Scandinavia Spain university visitors

1. state : president = city : mayor
2. Stockholm : Sweden = Madrid : ____________
3. stocking : foot = cap : ____________
4. story : to tell = song : to ____________
5. stranger : friend = alien : ____________
6. underground train : passengers = zoo : ____________
7. salt : salty = sugar : ____________
8. sure : unsure = to know : to ____________
9. swamp : humid = desert : ____________
10. Panama : Central America = Sweden : ____________
11. taxi driver : taxi = astronaut : ____________
12. teacher : school = professor : ____________
13. teacher : student = doctor : ____________
14. television : to switch off = window : to ____________
15. thin : fat = industrious : ____________
16. tiger : cat = wolf : ____________
17. to add : to subtract = to multiply : to ____________
18. to arrive : to depart = arrival : ____________
19. to attack : to defend = attack : ____________
20. to fall asleep : to wake up = to begin : to ____________

**Setzen Sie die Buchstaben in die richtige Reihenfolge, um die logische Entsprechung zu finden.**

**TEST 45**

1. fence : wood = wall : [ntose] stone
2. finger : ring = neck : [eakelccn] ____________
3. fire : ashes = cause : [etfcfe] ____________
4. fish : aquarium = cow : [narb] ____________
5. fish : gills = man : [ugsnl] ____________
6. fisherman : net = hunter : [ung] ____________
7. fishing rod : to fish = gun : [to ohtso] ____________
8. flour : bread = cocoa : [ltchcooae] ____________
9. flower : plant = fish : [nlmaai] ____________
10. foot : toe = hand : [irgfen] ____________
11. foreigner : visa = driver : [eciecnl] ____________
12. France : cognac = Russia : [okadv] ____________
13. frog : to jump = snake : to [lithsre] ____________
14. garbage : garbage can = cigarette : [hsrtaay] ____________
15. gardener : garden = cook : [cientkh] ____________
16. generous : thrifty = rich : [orpo] ____________
17. Germany : country = Berlin : [yitc] ____________
18. girl : boy = sister : [erthobr] ____________
19. glass : to break = bomb : [to xldoeep] ____________
20. gold : plastic = expensive : [hacpe] ____________

## TEST 46 Setzen Sie ein.

beautiful bicycle doctor early garage Germany hour in masterpiece parking passed song stomach Speak task there third ~~trusted~~ tune What

1. Man kann ihm zum Glück vertrauen. > Fortunately, he can be trusted.
2. Parken verboten! > No ___________!
3. das Instrument stimmen > to _______ an instrument
4. Was fehlt Ihnen? > _______ is wrong with you?
5. den Arzt holen > to call in the ___________
6. der/die/das Dritte > the _________
7. die deutsche Geschichte > the history of _____________
8. Sie hat die Prüfung bestanden / geschafft. > She ________ the examination.
9. Wie schön das ist! > How _________________!
10. ein Lied singen > to sing a _______
11. eine Aufgabe stellen > to set a _______
12. eine halbe Stunde > half an _______
13. am frühen Morgen / frühmorgens > _________ in the morning
14. Wo ist die nächste Autowerkstatt? > Where is the next __________?
15. Sprich lauter! > _________ up!
16. er hat ein Meisterwerk geschaffen > he has created a ____________________
17. erstens / an erster Stelle > ____ the first place
18. es ist niemand da > _________ is nobody there
19. etwas gegen Bauchweh > something for _____________ ache
20. aufs Rad steigen > to get on the _____________

**Finden Sie waagerecht oder senkrecht 38 positive Eigenschaften.**



| | | | | | | | | | | | | | | | | | |
|---|---|---|---|---|---|---|---|---|---|---|---|---|---|---|---|---|---|
| h | e | l | p | f | u | l | v | e | p | o | j | h | p | h | u | h | a |
| b | a | l | a | n | c | e | d | l | r | v | o | a | u | u | p | o | c |
| p | a | t | i | e | n | t | e | e | e | e | l | r | n | m | l | n | t |
| p | o | l | i | t | e | z | w | g | t | r | l | d | c | o | o | e | i |
| t | o | l | e | r | a | n | t | a | t | s | y | w | t | r | c | s | v |
| p | r | q | u | i | e | t | z | n | y | a | n | o | u | o | h | t | e |
| l | e | b | r | a | v | e | y | t | v | t | i | r | a | u | e | h | a |
| d | **s** | **y** | **m** | **p** | **a** | **t** | **h** | **e** | **t** | **i** | **c** | k | l | s | e | m | k |
| j | p | c | b | s | o | c | i | a | b | l | e | i | l | t | r | d | p |
| l | o | v | i | n | g | x | l | e | a | e | z | n | e | h | f | c | c |
| m | n | o | p | t | i | m | i | s | t | i | c | g | g | i | u | h | v |
| b | s | b | e | a | u | t | i | f | u | l | e | f | u | n | l | a | w |
| h | i | n | v | a | r | e | l | i | a | b | l | e | v | c | j | r | s |
| c | b | e | l | i | n | t | e | l | l | i | g | e | n | t | i | m | t |
| j | l | a | q | v | a | t | h | l | e | t | i | c | y | f | a | i | r |
| d | e | t | x | f | r | a | t | t | r | a | c | t | i | v | e | n | o |
| e | x | c | i | t | i | n | g | f | r | i | e | n | d | l | y | g | n |
| c | l | e | a | n | g | e | n | e | r | o | u | s | r | i | c | h | g |

# TEST 48 Kreuzworträtsel

**WAAGERECHT**

2 Y**, I work here.
4 They went to the o**** instead of to the theatre.
7 I have one s** and one daughter.
9 My c** has run out of petrol.
10 Spaghetti and macaroni are types of p****.
11 The criminal was executed on the electric c****.
12 Would you like some i** in your drink?
13 Should I d** my grey hair black?
14 He hurt his left e** and can't see very well.
15 We're seeing a classical play at the t******.
18 I a* at home today.
19 The Taj Mahal is in I****.
21 T**** are my shoes, those are yours.
23 I'd like some bread a** butter.

25 What did you s**?

27 The letter needs a s**** before you post it.

29 He's t**** after all the hard work.

30 Could I speak t* him?

31 She has everything under c******.

34 The children a** playing outside.

36 I hope you like the green p** soup.

38 The a** in the city is polluted.

39 She'd like to l**** Spanish.

40 The t**** pulled into the railway station.

41 The girl screamed into his e**.

42 T** food here is delicious.

43 Go a**** with the plan.

44 He's turned grey with a**.

**SENKRECHT**

1 His motorcycle is faster than my m****.

2 Y******** she was fine, but today she's ill.

3 I need a s**** to measure the weight.

4 We listened to the Philharmonic O******** playing.

5 Could you tell us the e**** price?

6 They signed an a******** to divide the land.

7 a typewriter key: s****

8 Her n**** and nephew are visiting her.

16 He h** a lot of money and is very powerful.

17 We take the dogs for a r** every evening.

19 The cat is lying in i** basket.

20 A******** is the home of the kangaroo.

22 I understood after he e******** it to me.

23 He loves flying an a********.

24 What d** you do yesterday evening?

26 That was a long time a**.

28 I'd like some beer, t**.

31 The restaurants on the c**** serve fresh fish.

32 The n**** will give you an injection.

33 Do you have to l**** already?

35 Do you have any e**** sheets of paper?

37 Don't a**** me with your questions!

## TEST 49 Setzen Sie ein.

advice break broken change ~~forward~~ Good if less light little make remember reserve school some soon thanks This would your

1. nach vorn > forward
2. ich erinnere mich, dass > I ______________ that
3. ich trinke lieber Wein als Bier > I _________ rather have wine than beer
4. schlimmstenfalls / im äußersten Fall > ____ the worst comes to the worst
5. Geld wechseln > to ___________ money
6. jemanden um Rat fragen > to ask someone's ___________
7. wenig Zeit > ___________ time
8. Der Schalter ist kaputt. > The switch is ___________.
9. sich den Arm brechen > to _________ one's arm
10. Biegen Sie nach der dritten Verkehrsampel rechts ab. > Turn to the right at the third traffic _________.
11. viel weniger > much _______
12. Dieser Mann ist verletzt. > _______ man is injured.
13. mit Dank annehmen > to accept with ___________
14. Viel Glück! > _______ luck!
15. glücklich machen > to _______ happy
16. immer der Nase nach > just follow _______ nose
17. in die Schule gehen > to go to ___________
18. so bald wie möglich > as _______ as possible
19. Bringen Sie mir bitte etwas Zitrone. > Can I have _______ lemon, please.
20. Es ist besser, eine Reservierung für die Tickets zu machen. > It is better to _________ the tickets.

## Finden Sie Wortpaare mit gegenteiliger Bedeutung.



calm covered drab gigantic ~~horizontal~~ illegal masculine optimistic permanent spiritual stingy tame unknown

1. vertical - horizontal
2. boisterous - ______
3. feminine - ______
4. pessimistic - ______
5. microscopic - ______
6. famous - ______
7. generous - ______
8. colorful - ______
9. wild - ______
10. bare - ______
11. legal - ______
12. temporary - ______
13. physical - ______

## TEST 51 Setzen Sie die Namen europäischer Länder ein.

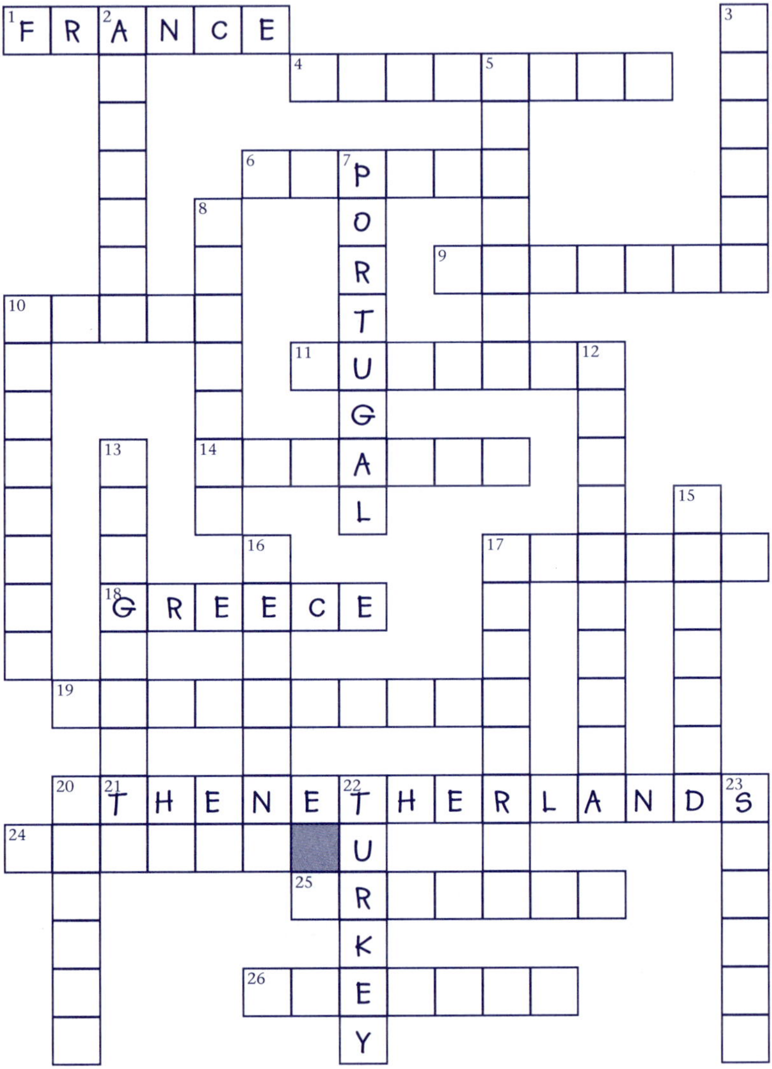

**Setzen Sie ein.**

beach ~~cards~~ contact country doctor eggs enough Have left look lose matches once out outside quarrel repair spoilt Shut want

1. Karten spielen > to play cards
2. das genügt völlig > that's quite ___________
3. Was willst du eigentlich? > What do you _______ anyway?
4. Hat man je so was gesehen? > _____ you ever seen such a thing?
5. Ich habe meine Kontaktlinsen verloren. > I have lost my _____________ lenses.
6. Ich möchte zwei Rühreier. > I would like two scrambled _______.
7. Meine linke Hand blutet. > My _______ hand is bleeding.
8. den Streit beilegen > to settle a _____________
9. die Milch ist verdorben / sauer > the milk has ___________
10. Sie müssen in drei Monaten wieder ausreisen. > You must leave the __________ again in three months.
11. ein für allemal > _______ and for all
12. eine Schachtel Streichhölzer > a box of _____________
13. einen Kranken pflegen > to _______ after a patient
14. das Hotel am Strand. > the hotel on the _________.
15. draußen geht ein Wind > there is a strong wind blowing _____________
16. arbeitslos sein > to be _____ of work
17. Tür zu! / Bitte die Tür schließen! > _______ the door, please!
18. Würden Sie das Auto reparieren? > Could you ___________ the car?
19. Rufen Sie einen Arzt. > Call a ___________.
20. aus den Augen verlieren > to _______ sight of

## TEST 53 Setzen Sie die Sätze in die richtige Reihenfolge.

◯ „But now I can't get it out of my head!"

◯ „Beware! If you think of noodle soup while you are digging, you won't find it."

◯ „Damn! I've never thought of noodle soup in my life!"

◯ „You'll find the treasure a few metres under the ground."

◯ „Take a spade with you and dig for treasure."

◯ „Wait for a clear night with a full moon and go to the old graveyard at midnight."

◯ „You will be very rich if you do exactly as I tell you."

◯ On a clear night with a full moon he goes to the graveyard and begins to dig.

(1) Peter goes to a fortune teller to ask about his future.

◯ Peter is excited about the treasure and buys himself a spade.

◯ She looks into a crystal ball for a long time and then tells him:

◯ Suddenly he throws down the spade and runs away:

**Setzen Sie die Buchstaben in die richtige Reihenfolge, um die logische Entsprechung zu finden.**



1. good : bad = advantage : [avneiadsdgat] disadvantage
2. good luck : bad luck = success : [ralfieu] ________________
3. gorilla : jungle = camel : [teersd] ________________
4. grapefruit : bitter = vinegar : [orsu] ________________
5. green : go = red : [ptos] ________________
6. group : individual = together : [nloea] ________________
7. guitar : trumpet = to strum : [to lwob] ________________
8. gun : bullet = bow : [orawr] ________________
9. hammer : nail = screwdriver : [ecswr] ________________
10. hand : glove = foot : [ehso] ________________
11. hands : to stroke = lips : [to isks] ________________
12. happiness : to laugh = unhappiness : [to ryc] ________________
13. head : heart = reason : [smotonie] ________________
14. hearing aid : to hear = spectacles : [to ese] ________________
15. heaven : hell = angel : [iedlv] ________________
16. Helsinki : Finland = Dublin : [lrnedal] ________________
17. train : conductor = aeroplane : [eswsaesdtr] ________________
18. house : homeless = work : [yndlmeoupe] ________________

## TEST 55 Setzen Sie ein.

banks best black cold else faintest fault first for from ~~May~~ of right same soul teeth these two welcome worse

1. Darf ich die Rechnung haben? > May I have the check?
2. ich friere / mich friert / mir ist kalt > I am ________
3. ich tu's trotzdem > I'll do it all the ________
4. schwarz auf weiß > in __________ and white
5. keiner von beiden > neither of the ______
6. sich die Zähne putzen > to brush one's __________
7. ich habe nicht die geringste Ahnung > I haven't got the __________ idea
8. willkommen heißen > to ______________
9. mit Leib und Seele > with heart and ________
10. Bitte bügeln Sie diese Anziehsachen / Kleidungsstücke. > Please iron __________ clothes.
11. immer schlechter > __________ and worse / from bad to worse
12. in diesem Augenblick > at the moment / ________ now
13. An wem liegt es? / Wer ist schuld? > Whose __________ is it?
14. golden / aus Gold > golden / made ____ gold
15. aus Deutschland > ________ Germany
16. sonst nichts > nothing ________
17. er tut sein Bestes > he does his ________
18. erstens / an erster Stelle > in the __________ place
19. das Ufer der Themse > the __________ of the River Thames
20. etwas gegen starke Zahnschmerzen > something ______ a bad toothache

1. Carbon is required for starting a fire. false
2. An emu is a bird. true
3. The Statue of Liberty is in New York. ________
4. Fish can live only in water. ________
5. The river Thames flows through London. ________
6. The heart has one valve. ________
7. Arabic is written from right to left. ________
8. Glass expands when heated. ________
9. Potatoes grow under the ground. ________
10. A rat is bigger than a mouse. ________
11. If you can't see things nearby you are short-sighted. ________
12. The Grand Canyon is in the eastern United States. ________
13. A leap year has three hundred sixty-six days. ________
14. French is not spoken in Canada. ________
15. America is named after Amerigo Vespucci. ________
16. Eighteen is a prime number. ________
17. The Mississippi is the broadest river in the world. ________
18. A cauliflower is a flower. ________
19. Mozart was a famous composer. ________
20. An ant is a big animal. ________

## Kreuzworträtsel

### WAAGERECHT

1 She loves listening to m****, especially jazz.
4 R** is the colour which denotes danger.
6 An a**** a day keeps the doctor away.
9 The i** on the lake is thick enough to skate on.
10 He put his a** around her.
11 The car won't start, something is wrong with the m****.
12 He's five years o**.
13 I s** your brother yesterday at the shopping centre.
15 Have you had enough, or would you like some m***?
16 An a***** is a type of nut.
18 Today is the 12** of July.
20 The h*** of the shoe came off.
21 W********* D.C. is the capital of the USA.

24 They did it by t*********, nobody helped them.

25 What is the exchange r*** of the dollar into the yen?

28 N*, I don't work here.

29 It's too hot to wear shoes, wear your s*****s.

31 She's a movie s***. She has acted in many films.

32 Please s** the carton down gently, it contains glass.

35 She was my classmate, but I don't know h** very well.

36 Would you like some French o**** soup?

37 I need not o**, but two new dresses.

38 He's blind in one e**, but can see well with the other.

39 W**** did you buy that from?

40 D** you meet him yesterday?

41 He drinks one l**** of juice a day.

**SENKRECHT**

1 'Sayonara' m**** 'Good bye' in Japanese.

2 The keys must be s********, but I can't find them!

3 Which movie is playing at the c***** tonight?

4 He's changed r********* since we met, I hardly know him.

5 I have a d*** with her at 8 p.m.

6 Eighteen people can fly in this a******* at a time.

7 The tourist took a p**** of the carvings.

8 Every e** marks a new beginning.

14 I a** pizza for lunch.

17 Can you d**** the tango?

19 He t********* to kill her son if she didn't comply.

20 She h**** him, but loves his brother.

22 We t******** the goods to the customer by ship.

23 How do you say 'breaded veal cutlet' in French? - E*******.

26 I got a blister on my right t** because of my new shoe.

27 She'd like to t***** all around the world.

30 He had the n**** to ask for a raise!

33 T**** are a lot of jobs vacant.

34 The windows are banging due to the w***.

35 Good morning, h** are you?

## TEST 58 Setzen Sie ein.

battery ~~by~~ Cheer his holds limit lot luck minute Open or pace party recommended sample shop taste took understands vanilla

1. Fahren wir mit dem Zug oder Auto? > Shall we go _by_ train or car?
2. das kostet viel Geld > that will cost a ______ of money
3. Ich liebe Vanilleeis. > I love ______________ ice cream.
4. Schritt halten mit > to keep ________ with
5. der Saal fasst neunzig Personen > the hall __________ ninety people
6. Verkäuferin gesucht > ________ assistant wanted
7. Ihre Firma wurde uns durch ... empfohlen. > Your company was ______________________ to us by ... .
8. Die Batterie ist entladen. > The ______________ is weak.
9. Sie machte ein Foto von ihm. > She _________ a picture of him.
10. Wie heißt er doch gleich? > What's ______ name again?
11. Sie versteht sehr wenig Englisch. > She ______________________ very little English.
12. Hier öffnen! > ________ here!
13. Ein Muster finden Sie in der Anlage. > Please find enclosed a ____________.
14. Wir hatten eine schöne Geburtstagsfeier. > We had a nice birthday __________.
15. bitter schmecken > to ____________ bitter
16. alles hat seine Grenzen > there is a __________ to everything
17. Glück bringen > to bring good ________
18. Möchten Sie lieber eine Cola oder ein Bier? > Would you like a coke ____ a beer?
19. Kopf hoch! / Nur Mut! > __________ up!
20. auf die Minute > to the ____________

**Finden Sie die logische Entsprechung.**

air bedroom country guilt legs loud oral pages park pavement permission refuse river ~~sailor~~ seal shell victory work worthless

1. to command : to obey = captain : sailor
2. to cook : kitchen = to sleep : ________
3. to swim : water = to fly : ________
4. to drive : road = to walk : ________
5. to forbid : to allow = ban : ________
6. to lose : to win = loss : ________
7. yes : no = to accept : to ________
8. to sign : signature = to stamp : ________
9. to write : to speak = written : ________
10. treasure : valuable = garbage : ________
11. tree : bark = egg : ________
12. tree : leaves = book : ________
13. shirt : sleeves = trousers : ________
14. university : to study = factory : to ________
15. victim : perpetrator = innocence : ________
16. villa : to live = parking place : to ________
17. village : city = stream : ________
18. violin : drum = soft : ________
19. violin : musical instrument = Italy : ________

## TEST 60 Finden Sie Wortpaare mit gegenteiliger Bedeutung.

allow answer arrive close decrease defend destroy die end go hate ~~lose~~ obey punish reap receive sell

1. to win - to lose
2. to live - to ______
3. to love - to ______
4. to buy - to ______
5. to depart - to ______
6. to forbid - to ______
7. to attack - to ______
8. to come - to ______
9. to command - to ______
10. to begin - to ______
11. to question - to ______
12. to build - to ______
13. to reward - to ______
14. to increase - to ______
15. to send - to ______
16. to sow - to ______
17. to open - to ______

**Setzen Sie ein.**

accompanied anything asleep come day example fall ~~going~~ hold kind knotty nothing notebook open other place quite swim take weather

1. ich gehe (die Treppe) hinunter > I am _going_ downstairs
2. ich weiß nichts davon > I don't know __________ about it
3. schwimmen gehen > to go for a ______
4. sich festhalten an > to ______ fast to
5. nichts Schlimmes > __________ serious
6. ein Beispiel geben > to give an __________
7. ein schwieriger Punkt > a _________ problem
8. eine ganze Weile > _______ a while
9. eingeschlafen sein > to have fallen _________
10. mit anderen Worten > in _______ words
11. in Begleitung von > ________________ by
12. in ein Heft schreiben > to write in a ____________
13. von Tag zu Tag > from _____ to day
14. krank werden > to ______ ill
15. große Augen machen > to ______ one's eyes wide
16. erstens / an erster Stelle > in the first _______
17. heute ist schönes Wetter > the _____ is fine today
18. etwas zur Kenntnis nehmen > to ______ note of
19. zu Ende gehen > to ______ to an end
20. tun Sie mir den Gefallen > be so ______ as to

## TEST 62 Stimmt das?

1. Cakes are made of flour, eggs, sugar and butter. true
2. Nylon is a synthetic fibre. ________
3. Zoology is the study of plants. false
4. Like poles attract. ________
5. Canada is the largest country in North America. ________
6. The moon is bigger than the sun. ________
7. Antartica lies at the North Pole. ________
8. Coffee contains caffeine. ________
9. The capital of Australia is Melbourne. ________
10. The United States have a larger population than Canada. ________
11. Ornithology is the study of birds. ________
12. The second World War began in 1945. ________
13. Diamonds are found in mines. ________
14. The brother of my father is my brother-in-law. ________
15. The cougar is a fish. ________
16. The Sun revolves around the Earth. ________
17. French, Spanish and Romanian are romanic languages. ________
18. Oil is lighter than water. ________
19. Loch Ness is in Scotland. ________
20. Light travels faster than sound. ________

**Setzen Sie ein.**



away cannot damaged does engine glass late light nice room Should ~~serve~~ take too way weekend When Where wood your

1. Haben Sie Kinderportionen? > Do you _serve_ children's portions?
2. Wann sind Sie geboren? > _______ were you born?
3. Das Fahrzeug ist beschädigt. > The vehicle is ____________.
4. das Wochenende verbringen > to spend the ____________
5. Ich möchte ein Einzelzimmer mit Dusche. > I would like a single _______ with a shower.
6. Licht machen > to switch on the _________
7. Die Maschine verbraucht zuviel Strom. > This machine uses _____ much electricity.
8. Sie dürfen den Wagen hier nicht stehenlassen. > You __________ leave the car here.
9. Wie nett! > How _______!
10. Bitte nehmen Sie mein Gepäck. > Please _________ my luggage / baggage.
11. am späten Nachmittag > in the _______ afternoon
12. Entschuldigen Sie! / Entschuldigung! > I beg _______ pardon! / (I am) sorry!
13. Wo kann ich Briefmarken kaufen? > _________ can I buy stamps?
14. Sollen wir in den Zoo oder ins Museum gehen? > __________ we go to the zoo or the museum?
15. Holz hacken > to chop _______
16. Fort! / Verschwinde! / Raus! > Go _______!
17. Irgend etwas stimmt nicht mit dem Motor. > There is something wrong with the __________.
18. Auf welche Weise? > In what _____?
19. Nur die Ruhe! / Immer mit der Ruhe! > Easy ____ it! / Take it easy!
20. aus Glas > made of _________

 Kreuzworträtsel

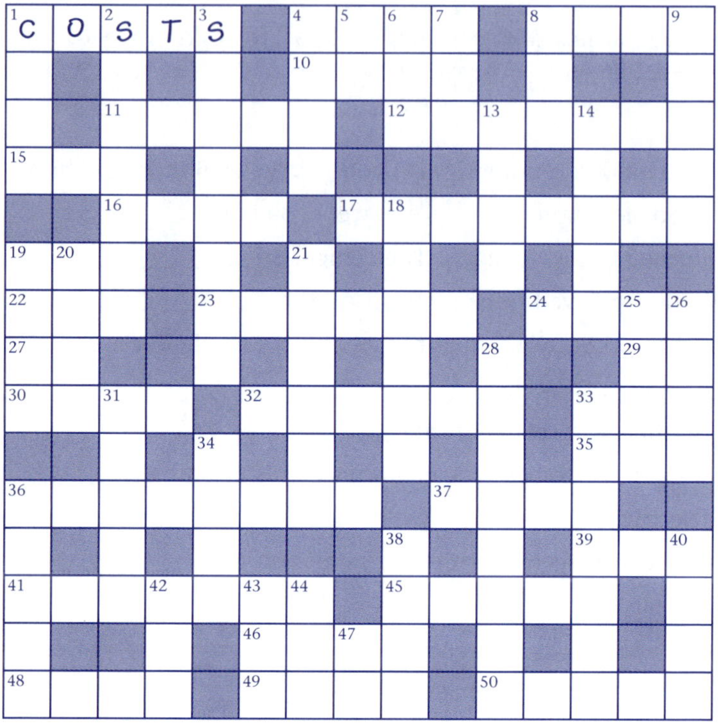


## WAAGERECHT

1 The beer c**** $3.

4 T*** is a nasty remark!

8 I hate working for my b***.

10 Come h*** at once!

11 The singer has a beautiful v****.

12 I was promoted to m****** from assistant manager.

15 The blind cannot s**.

16 What's your n***?

17 You need a s******* at the beach in summer.

19 Summers in tropical countries are very h**.

22 Do you have a** cigars?

23 Use the n***** to wipe your mouth.

24 The businessmen struck a d*** after much negotiation.

27 I* is hot today!

29 S* what?

30 The bank will give you a l***.

32 I c***** swim.

33 S** down!

35 She h** three dogs.

36 He is c*******, he is always losing things.

37 Let's go i*** the house. It's getting cold.

39 R** is cheaper than whisky.

41 Wrap the food in t******, it will stay fresh.

45 The walls need a fresh coat of p****.

46 I have no t*** to meet you.

48 H*** the picture on the wall.

49 Have you s*** the movie?

50 There are 12 g**** and 15 boys in the class.

**SENKRECHT**

1 The c*** grazed in the pasture.

2 He is s****** years old, but in good health.

3 The children are s******* in the pool.

4 The grapes are good, buy t***.

5 H* is an excellent driver.

6 Put your a** around me. Hug me!

7 T** is cheaper than coffee.

8 She is wearing a lacy b**.

9 The tennis player has a fast s****.

13 I have a runny n***, pass me a tissue.

14 Wine is fermented g**** juice.

18 The workers have joined various trade u*****.

19 The garden was covered with h*** stones after the storm.

20 He got o*** the train.

21 He s***** fluent English.

25 Singapore is in A***.

26 The millionaire has l*** of money.

28 I hate s******* in queues.

31 The cook wears an a**** in the kitchen.

33 Though tall, she is s****** then her husband.

34 I would a*** like to see the movie.

36 Don't c**** a cold!

38 O*** the window, it is stuffy in here.

40 This room is an absolute m***. Clean it up!

42 London is sometimes blanketed by thick f**.

43 The dog wants i** food.

44 Never l** in court.

47 Can you help m*?

**Finden Sie die logische Entsprechung.**



address arrogance books button candle ~~compartment~~ Dollar East furniture gas horse length orange pointed rice snow vase week write

1. house : room = train : compartment
2. humble : arrogant = humility : ______
3. house : light = hut : ______
4. ice skates : ice = skis : ______
5. iron : metal = oxygen : ______
6. Italy : spaghetti = China : ______
7. jacket : clothing = sofa : ______
8. jacket : zipper = shirt : ______
9. January : year = Monday : ______
10. Japan : Yen = USA : ______
11. juice : bottle = flowers : ______
12. kilo : weight = meter : ______
13. kiosk : newspapers = bookstore : ______
14. knife : sharp = needle : ______
15. knife : to cut = pencil : to ______
16. lamb : sheep = foal : ______
17. left : right = West : ______
18. lemon : yellow = orange : ______
19. telephone : telephone number = letter : ______

## TEST 66 Setzen Sie die Sätze in die richtige Reihenfolge.

◯ "And what does the third guy do?" the passer-by wants to know.

◯ "He puts the lanterns in the holes, but today he is ill."

◯ "There are normally three of us."

◯ A passer-by observes this happening.

◯ He asks them why they're doing that and the men explain it to him.

(1) Two men are working on a road.

◯ One of them digs a hole.

◯ The other immediately fills it up.

◯ This happens a number of times.

**Setzen Sie ein.**



another class danger deal do fun great green just latest news nice says seize ship short ~~sing~~ soap takes tap

1. falsch singen > to sing out of tune
2. ich glaube es ihm > I believe what he _______
3. ich wollte gerade weggehen > I was _______ about to leave
4. sehr viel > a great _______ of
5. den Hahn zudrehen > to turn off the _____
6. sich lustig machen über > to make _____ of
7. die Gelegenheit ergreifen > to _________ the opportunity
8. die neuesten Nachrichten > the ___________ news
9. ein Stück Seife > a bar of _______
10. eine Neuigkeit erfahren > to hear a piece of _______
11. einen Dienst erweisen / einen Gefallen tun > to ___________ a service
12. mit dem Schiff fahren > to travel by _______
13. in Gefahr > in ___________
14. in großen Mengen > in _________ quantities
15. noch ein Brot > _____________ loaf of bread
16. er sorgt für die Familie > he _________ care of the family
17. erster Klasse > first-_________
18. grün anstreichen > to paint it _________
19. heute ist schönes Wetter > the weather is _______ today
20. kurz vorher > a _________ while ago

## TEST 68

**Setzen Sie Verwandtschaftsbezeichnungen ein.**
**Welches Lösungswort ergibt sich in der senkrechten Reihe?**

| | | | | | | | | | | | | |
|---|---|---|---|---|---|---|---|---|---|---|---|---|
| | | | | | **G** | R | | N | D | S | | N |
| S | | S | T | | **R** | | | | | | | |
| | | | | | | | N | T | | | | |
| | | | | | **N** | | | C | | | | |
| | | | | | **D** | | | G | H | T | | R |
| | | | | | **M** | | T | H | | R | | |
| | | | | S | | N | | | | | | |
| | | | | | **T** | W | | N | S | | | |
| | | N | | P | **H** | | W | | | | | |
| | | N | C | L | | | | | | | | |
| F | | T | H | | **R** | | | | | | | |

1. Beethoven was a German author. false
2. The Niagara Falls are on the U.S.- Canadian border. true
3. Bees live in a hive. _________
4. A pentagon has 6 sides. _________
5. Rain comes from clouds. _________
6. Switzerland is a land-locked country. _________
7. A mile is equal to 1.6 kilometers. _________
8. Egypt is famous for pyramids. _________
9. Australia is the smallest continent in the world. _________
10. Water turns to ice at 0 degrees Celsius. _________
11. The Concorde jet is faster than the speed of sound. _________
12. Saturn is the smallest planet in our solar system. _________
13. Alexander Graham Bell invented the telephone. _________
14. Smoking causes lung disease. _________
15. Coconuts grow in cold climates. _________
16. The moon affects the tide at sea. _________
17. Greenland is the largest island in the world. _________
18. Mount Kilimanjaro is the highest mountain in the world. _____
19. One kilogram is equal to 2.2 pounds. _________
20. Steffi Graf is a Canadian tennis player. _________

## TEST 70 Setzen Sie ein.

campsite complaint customs Dutch early elections ~~got~~ listen make matter meaning ninety sooner speak Spanish this thousands

1. Haben Sie einen Feuerlöscher? > Have you _got_ a fire extinguisher?
2. Radio hören > to ___________ to the radio
3. Das ist eine gute Gelegenheit, Geld zu verdienen. > This is a good opportunity to __________ money.
4. Was soll das heißen? > What is the _____________ of this?
5. Tausende von Menschen > _________________ of people
6. über kurz oder lang / früher oder später > ___________ or later
7. Ich fahre morgen sehr früh ab. > I am leaving _________ tomorrow morning.
8. Es gibt keine Demokratie ohne freie Wahlen. > There is no democracy without free ___________.
9. Mein Großvater ist neunzig. > My grandfather is ___________.
10. Besorg mir einen Übersetzer für Spanisch-Holländisch. > Get me an interpreter for Spanish-_________.
11. Die Sache ist erledigt! > That settles the ___________!
12. Sie müssen Zoll zahlen. > You will have to pay _____________ duties.
13. Wir haben Ihre Reklamation erhalten. > We confirm receipt of your _________________.
14. Bitte sprechen Sie langsam. > Please _________ slowly.
15. sieh dir das an > look at _______
16. Er machte die Übersetzung vom Spanischen ins Englische. > He did a translation from _____________ into English.
17. Ist hier ein Campingplatz in der Nähe? > Is there a _______ close by?

**Setzen Sie die Buchstaben in die richtige Reihenfolge, um die gegenteilige Bedeutung zu finden.**



1. export - [tmorpi] import
2. love - [eath] ____________
3. guest - [tohs] ____________
4. heat - [dolc] ____________
5. depth - [etgihh ] ____________
6. length - [tarhdeb] ____________
7. life - [tehda] ____________
8. hunger - [trhtsi] ____________
9. poverty - [shirec] ____________
10. student - [eechtar] ____________
11. friend - [nmeye] ____________
12. summer - [rtinwe] ____________
13. heaven - [ellh] ____________
14. angel - [eivld] ____________
15. day - [hitgn] ____________
16. west - [tase] ____________
17. minority - [iaoyrmjt] ____________
18. lies - [trhtu] ____________
19. marriage - [cioerdv] ____________
20. happiness - [sandsse] ____________

## TEST 72 Kreuzworträtsel

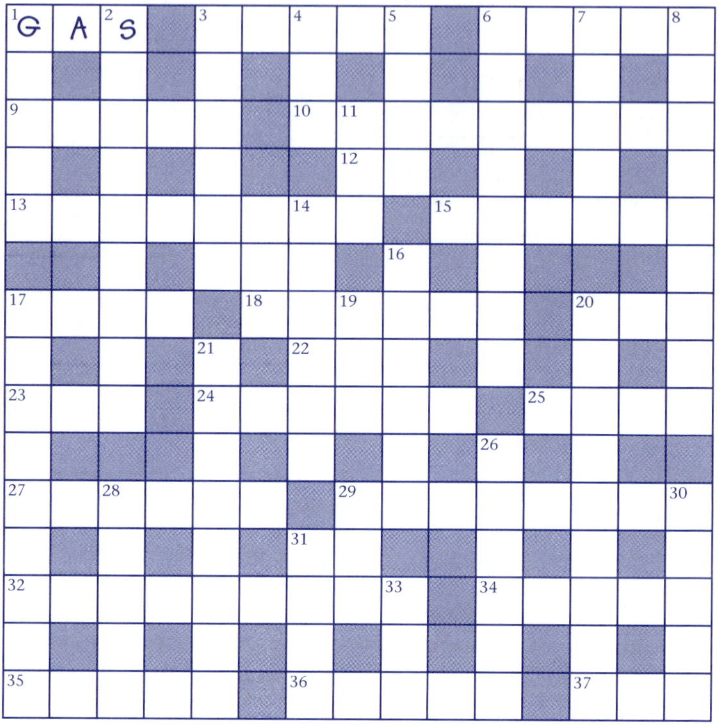


### WAAGERECHT

1 We need to fill the car up with g**.

3 Dublin is an I**** city.

6 New Delhi is the capital of I****.

9 The road a**** is closed for repairs.

10 Could I borrow your pencil s********?

12 He works a* home.

13 The house is s******* on the banks of a river.

15 Delphi is in G*****.

17 The swimming p*** is dirty.

18 Meet me b***** you leave.

20 Steak and kidney p** for me, please.

22 Bring up a v** of wine from the cellar.

23 We're staying at a quiet country i**.

24 She has a very p***** face.

25 This s*** is reserved.

27 I need a can o***** to open the can.

29 I prefer l******* to orangeade.

31 Did he really say s*?

32 Take the I******** express from Frankfurt to Geneva.

34 She's d**** something important, please don't disturb her.

35 The palace is really g****, with gold carvings and antique furniture.

36 Could you e**** this data into the computer?

37 G** well soon!

**SENKRECHT**

1 The church has stained g**** windows.

2 The s******** soup is delicious, the corn must have been fresh.

3 Mahatma Gandhi was an I*****.

4 The dog buried i** bone in the garden.

5 The food is cold, let's h*** it up.

6 This isn't made here, it's i******* from Japan.

7 She loves to d**** at the disco.

8 They finally reached an a******** after hours of discussion.

11 He h** a fever and couldn't work.

14 I'll see you at e***** a.m.

16 Let's take him a b***** of champagne!

17 She's ill with food p********.

19 He's too f**, he has to lose weight.

20 They're p******** the house for the arrival of their guests.

21 A genie a******* out of the magic lamp.

26 We need to buy some washing p*****.

28 The additional part will cost you 24 $ e****.

29 Thanks a l** for your help.

30 She owns e**** pairs of jeans.

31 That shoe isn't available in your s***.

33 We haven't y** received your letter.

## TEST 73 Setzen Sie ein.

attend break comfort extent general get glass goes loss metres minutes ~~number~~ regards shoes small speak step there train understand

1. falsch verbunden > wrong number
2. das ist kein Trost für mich > that's no ____________ to me
3. laut sprechen > to ________ in a loud voice
4. ich habe das Wort nicht verstanden > I didn't ________________ the word
5. den Zug nehmen / mit der Bahn fahren > to take a ________
6. die Schuhe anziehen > to put on one's ________
7. ein leichter Fehler > a __________ mistake
8. eine Versammlung besuchen > to __________ a meeting
9. einen Verlust erleiden > to suffer a _______
10. Sie haben 13 Stunden ohne Pause gearbeitet. > They worked 13 hours without a _______.
11. im Allgemeinen > in ____________
12. in Not geraten / in Schwierigkeiten kommen > to _____ into trouble
13. in hohem Maße > to a large __________
14. dreizehn Meter lang > thirteen __________ long
15. grüßen Sie ihn von mir > give him my ____________
16. es bleiben zwei übrig > ________ are two left
17. es ist selbstverständlich, dass > it _______ without saying that
18. auf Schritt und Tritt > at every _______ / at every turn
19. nur noch 3 Minuten > only 3 ____________ left
20. aus einem Glas trinken > to drink out of a ________

**Finden Sie waagerecht oder senkrecht 28 Kleidungsstücke.**

| | | | | | | | | | | | | | | | |
|---|---|---|---|---|---|---|---|---|---|---|---|---|---|---|---|
| P | Q | C | U | N | D | E | R | S | H | I | R | T | K | W | Z |
| Q | B | A | D | R | E | S | S | S | W | E | A | T | E | R | B |
| I | E | P | Y | A | G | L | O | V | E | S | Z | J | J | H | L |
| W | G | C | O | S | T | U | M | E | S | A | S | D | P | N | O |
| S | X | W | X | B | S | O | C | K | S | S | E | E | U | Y | U |
| T | W | V | E | S | T | F | E | A | P | R | O | N | L | G | S |
| D | Q | Y | O | T | I | G | H | T | S | O | S | E | L | I | E |
| C | I | S | H | O | E | S | Y | F | W | O | S | G | O | G | G |
| B | R | A | S | S | I | E | R | E | C | V | A | D | V | Y | G |
| S | F | B | B | O | T | **S** | **U** | **S** | **P** | **E** | **N** | **D** | **E** | **R** | **S** |
| F | K | O | E | P | I | K | S | W | F | R | D | A | R | J | H |
| I | M | O | L | E | E | P | K | X | S | C | A | R | F | A | A |
| Q | O | T | T | K | Y | X | I | H | Z | O | L | S | H | C | T |
| N | Y | S | V | G | E | D | R | M | R | A | S | L | L | K | Q |
| Y | B | O | M | S | U | I | T | Y | B | T | U | I | P | E | J |
| A | V | G | T | R | O | U | S | E | R | S | C | P | T | T | A |

## TEST 75 Finden Sie die logische Entsprechung.

aquarium bald ~~bank~~ blood books Catholic daily day divorce drunk Denmark end fuel interest many match see single smoke whisper

1. letter : post office = money : bank
2. video store : videos = library : ____________
3. light : light switch = candle : ____________
4. lion : cage = fish : ____________
5. liqueur : to drink = tobacco : to ____________
6. Lisbon : Portugal = Copenhagen : ____________
7. lots : nothing = hairy : ____________
8. loud : soft = to scream : to ____________
9. love : end = marriage : ____________
10. lungs : air = heart : ____________
11. Luther : Protestant = Pope : ____________
12. magazine : newspaper = weekly : ____________
13. person : food = motor : ____________
14. marriage : children = capital : ____________
15. groom : bachelor = married : ____________
16. microphone : to speak = binoculars : to ____________
17. mineral water : sober = alcohol : ____________
18. minority : majority = few : ____________
19. moon : night = sun : ____________
20. morning : evening = beginning : ____________

**Setzen Sie ein.**

## TEST 76

calculation call contract first fortunately fried from Hold hurry keep name number pardon put repaired school ~~speaking~~ Step successful when

1. Hallo, wer ist dort? / Wer ist am Apparat? > Who is speaking?
2. Ich habe es eilig. > I'm in a ________.
3. Ich möchte zwei Spiegeleier. > I would like two ________ eggs.
4. Schieb die Schuld nicht auf mich! > Don't ______ the blame on me!
5. Geh zur Seite! > ________ aside!
6. sein Versprechen halten > to ________ one's promise
7. Der Elektriker hat die Sicherung repariert. > The electrician ______________ the fuse.
8. Bestellen Sie mir bitte ein Taxi. > Please get / ________ me a taxi.
9. sich unterscheiden von > to differ ________
10. Wir haben den Vertrag unterschrieben. > We signed the ________
11. Wie heißen Sie? / Wie ist Ihr Name? > What's your ________?
12. Sie sind bei rotem Licht über die Kreuzung gefahren. > You drove across the intersection ________ the lights were red.
13. Mit Ihrer Berechnung sind wir nicht einverstanden. > We are not in agreement with your __________________.
14. Bleiben Sie am Apparat! > ________ the line!
15. ich bitte Sie um Verzeihung > I beg your __________
16. Unterricht haben > to be at __________
17. Können Sie mich mit dieser Nummer verbinden? > Can you connect me to this __________?
18. vor allen Dingen > ________ of all
19. Erfolg haben > to be ________________
20. zum Glück > __________________

## TEST 77 Stimmt das?

1. An hour has three thousand six hundred seconds. true
2. A spider has 6 legs. false
3. Finnish, Hungarian and Estonian are related. ________
4. The capital of the United Kingdom is Glasgow. ________
5. My nephew is the daughter of my sister. ________
6. George Washington was the first President of the United States. ________
7. Shakespeare was an English playwright. ________
8. The capital of Switzerland is Geneva. ________
9. Tigers are found in Africa. ________
10. A football team consists of 10 players. ________
11. A tulip is a flower. ________
12. A glacier consists of ice. ________
13. The United States of America consists of 52 States. ________
14. One cannot see clearly in fog. ________
15. Kangaroos are found only in Australia. ________
16. Copper is a conductor of electricity. ________
17. Hollywood is in California. ________
18. Heavy rains cause earthquakes. ________
19. My wife's mother is my mother-in-law. ________
20. New Zealand is a part of Australia. ________

**Setzen Sie ein.**

abroad are born dig everything from gone good hard in just paper prefer reckon repaired saying stop ~~thank~~ ticket train

1. dafür danke ich Ihnen > I thank you for that
2. das sieht ihm ähnlich > that's ______ like him
3. ich habe den Zug verpasst > I've missed the ________
4. der Zug hält nicht > the train will not ______
5. fern der Heimat > far ______ home
6. die Zeitung lesen > to read the ________
7. lieber wollen > to __________
8. ein Loch graben > to _____ a hole
9. eine Eintrittskarte lösen > to buy a __________
10. eine schwere Arbeit > ______ work
11. Wir rechnen mit einer Lieferzeit von 8 Tagen. > We __________ on a delivery time of 8 days.
12. alles hat seine Grenzen > there is a limit to _________________
13. im Bett liegen > to be ___ bed
14. etwas in Reparatur geben / reparieren lassen > to have something ______
15. ins Ausland reisen > to go __________
16. er ist weg / er ist auf und davon > he has ______
17. es bleiben zwei übrig > there _____ two left
18. es ist selbstverständlich, dass > it goes without __________ that
19. geboren werden / auf die Welt kommen > to be ______
20. gut riechen > to smell ______

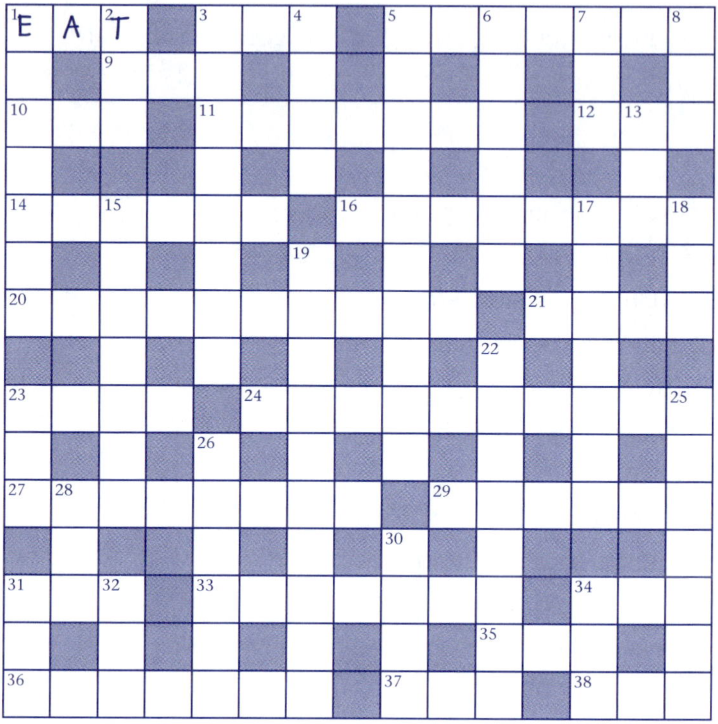

## WAAGERECHT

1 I'd like to e** a pizza today.

3 Could I have a glass of t** water, please.

5 He's wearing a gold e****** in his ear.

9 He called a little while a**.

10 I'd like a boiled e** for breakfast.

11 Could I have a blue pen i****** of the red pen?

12 Please s** down.

14 The thieves r***** the house.

16 Her nylon s******* has a ladder / run (am.) in it.

20 My watch is w*********, I can swim with it.

21 He's an e*** man, he likes to see people suffer.

23 The captain and his c*** were all safe.

24 I got an i********* to the party tomorrow.
27 He used his p******* to slice the cheese.
29 The bunkers are the s***** place during war.
31 They placed a b** on the horse races.
33 Go to an ear specialist for your e****** before the pain increases.
34 That costs 25 dollars p** person.
35 He can't s** without his spectacles.
36 They d****** formally for dinner.
37 Why did you d** your hair blue?
38 Did you get a** my messages?

**SENKRECHT**

1 She plucked her e****** with tweezers.
2 Check the price t** on the product.
3 This row is for t******* items like soap, shampoo, etc.
4 Did you p*** the letter in time?
5 We sell e********* items like computers, etc.
6 We must r***** our expenses to stay competitive.
7 A bird will attack i** reflection in a mirror.
8 Could you g** me a tea, please.
13 We're staying at an old i**.
15 He's available b****** 5 and 6 p.m.
17 Customers must pay their i****** immediately.
18 He uses g** to slick his hair back.
19 He has been t********* to another department.
22 The J******* are known for their politeness.
23 I like his new baseball c**.
25 This is a n****** product, it has no chemicals.
26 He never knocks before he e***** a room.
28 Look me in the e** when you speak to me!
30 I*** lemonade tastes great in the summer.
31 Today was a b** day for me, everything went wrong.
32 Do t** your shoe laces or you'll trip and fall.
34 Do you like the story of the „Princess and the p**"?.

## TEST 80 Setzen Sie Begriffe aus dem Bereich der Körperpflege ein. Welches Lösungswort ergibt sich in der senkrechten Reihe?

| | | | | | | | | | | | | |
|---|---|---|---|---|---|---|---|---|---|---|---|---|
| | | | B | R | | S | **H** | | | | | |
| | | | | | S | | | P | | | | |
| | | | | S | P | | **N** | G | | | | |
| | | | | P | | W | **D** | | R | | | |
| L | | P | S | T | | C | **K** | | | | | |
| | | | | T | | W | | L | | | | |
| | S | C | | S | S | | **R** | S | | | | |
| | | | | | | | **C** | | M | B | | |
| | | | M | | | T | **H** | W | | S | H | |
| | | | | | | M | | R | R | | R | |
| | | | | | T | W | | | Z | | R | S |
| | | | | P | | R | **F** | | M | | | |

## Finden Sie Wortpaare mit gegenteiliger Bedeutung.



1. bride - [roogm] groom
2. husband - [eifw ] ____________________
3. grandfather - [ertmnarhgdo] ____________________
4. son - [rgatdheu] ____________________
5. brother - [ritess] ____________________
6. uncle - [tuan] ____________________
7. nephew - [ciene] ____________________
8. widower - [iowwd] ____________________
9. gentleman - [yadl] ____________________
10. grandson - [eudnrhdgaragt] ____________________
11. morning - [vnngiee] ____________________
12. war - [ceepa] ____________________
13. old age - [otyhu] ____________________
14. departure - [iarvarl] ____________________
15. patient - [rotodc] ____________________
16. entrance - [txie] ____________________

## TEST 82 Setzen Sie ein.

after arm bottom capacity cheques day duty from great injured insured lend list ~~lot~~ mail park rather shipment truth vicinity

1. viel Lärm machen > to make a lot of noise
2. Ich kann meinen rechten Arm nicht bewegen. > I cannot move my right ______.
3. Nehmen Sie Schecks an? > Do you take ______________?
4. seine Pflicht verletzen > to fail in one's ________
5. Seine intellektuellen Fähigkeiten sind toll. > His intellectual ___________ is great.
6. Der Laden ist ganztägig geöffnet. > The shop is open all ______ long.
7. Kannst du mir deinen Stift leihen? > Can you _____ me your pen?
8. offen gestanden > to tell the __________
9. Ihre Sendung habe ich erhalten. > Your ____________ has arrived.
10. Gibt es ein Einkaufszentrum in der näheren Umgebung? > Is there a shopping centre in the ________________?
11. sicher vor / geschützt gegen > safe ________
12. Hier in der Nähe gibt es einen bewachten Parkplatz. > There is a supervised car-________ near here.
13. Dieser Mann ist verletzt. > This man is ______________.
14. Sind Sie haftpflichtversichert? > Are you __________ for third party risks?
15. mit großer Mühe > with __________ difficulty
16. unten auf der Seite > at the ____________ of the page
17. vor / während / nach den Mahlzeiten > before / during / __________ meals
18. Bringen Sie mir die Weinkarte. > Can I have the wine ________, please.
19. Es ist ziemlich riskant. > It is _________ risky.
20. zur Post bringen / aufgeben > to ________ / to post

**Finden Sie die logische Entsprechung.**

aunt Asia China Europe nest nutcracker painter painting poet quiet read sometimes son ~~sunset~~ sweet team vegetable young

1. morning : evening = sunrise : sunset
2. Moscow : Russia = Beijing : ____________________
3. mother : daughter = father : ____________________
4. mouse : hole = bird : ____________________
5. Mozart : music = Picasso : ____________________
6. music : composer = poem : ____________________
7. musician : orchestra = footballer : ____________________
8. sing : paint = singer : ____________________
9. mustard : hot = sugar : ____________________
10. nephew : niece = uncle : ____________________
11. never : seldom = always : ____________________
12. music : to listen to = newspaper : to ____________________
13. Nigeria : Africa = Vietnam : ____________________
14. Nile : Africa = Rhine : ____________________
15. noise : silence = loud : ____________________
16. can : can opener = nut : ____________________
17. old man : old = baby : ____________________
18. orange : fruit = cucumber : ____________________

# TEST 84 Kreuzworträtsel

## WAAGERECHT

1 I have nothing a****** him.

5 Please give us an i****** reply.

9 They have t** children, a boy and a girl.

10 C****** used to be a part of Yugoslavia.

11 That's a l**! I never took the money.

12 This c***** was built by a king in the 15th century.

14 Please sign this d*******.

17 One can pay by E********* in Europe.

18 A democracy must have a f*** press.

20 These roses are p***, not red.

21 He watches the soap opera on t********* .

24 I'd like an o******* with 2 eggs.

25 The children have l***** the alphabet.

27 Let's e**, I'm hungry.

29 Beijing is a C****** city.

30 The two countries are always at w** with each other.

31 His face is s****** due to mumps.

32 The sandwiches are packed in t****** so they won't spoil.

**SENKRECHT**

1 Did you read the a****** about cancer in the newspaper?

2 We lived there many years a**.

3 She's wearing a diamond n*******.

4 What t*** you so long?

5 He i********* her to me.

6 Have you visited the S***** of Liberty ?

7 A** of us are going to the party.

8 There's an interesting play at the t****** this week.

13 Isn't his behaviour s****** and unusual?

15 I called e****** this evening, but you weren't home.

16 This is a p********* zone, no vehicles are allowed.

19 She's n******* years old, next year she'll be twenty.

20 The computer can p****** a lot of data.

22 This juice has no preservatives, it is n******.

23 Please sharpen my p***** for me.

26 How much r*** do you pay for your flat?

28 He's t** lazy to do any work.

30 W** is that good-looking man?

## TEST 85 Setzen Sie ein.

afternoon country course fall gloves good ground hospital late left ~~miss~~ next savings step switch understand weakness well wood work

1. das Ziel verfehlen > to miss the mark
2. ich habe es nicht verstanden > I did not ________________
3. den Motor abstellen > to __________ off the engine
4. die Handschuhe anziehen > to put on one's __________
5. Wie lange halten Sie sich in diesem Land auf? > How long are you staying in this ___________?
6. dieser Anzug sitzt gut > this suit fits _______
7. Sie hat ihre ganzen Ersparnisse aufgebraucht. > She has used up all her ________.
8. eine Schwäche haben für > to have a _____________ for
9. einen Kurs besuchen / an einem Kurs teilnehmen > to attend a __________
10. fleißig arbeiten > to _______ hard
11. im Erdgeschoss > on the __________ floor
12. am späten Nachmittag > in the late _______________
13. in Stücke gehen / springen > to _______ to pieces
14. ins Krankenhaus bringen / schaffen > to take to ______________
15. Wo ist die nächste Werkstatt? > Where is the _______ repair service / garage?
16. Vorsicht, Stufe! > Mind the _______!
17. es bleiben zwei übrig > there are two _______
18. es ist spät > it's _______
19. aus Holz > made of _______
20. gut zu Fuß sein > to be a _______ walker

## Was passt zusammen?
## Bilden Sie Sprichwörter oder Redensarten.



| | | | |
|---|---|---|---|
| **1.** | Money makes | **a)** | a thorn. |
| **2.** | Never look a gift horse | **b)** | in his own country. |
| **3.** | No man is a prophet | **c)** | in the mouth. |
| **4.** | No rose without | **d)** | makes a thief. |
| **5.** | No sweet without | **e)** | never dies. |
| **6.** | Old love | **f)** | not make a summer. |
| **7.** | One does not wash | **g)** | one's dirty linen in public. |
| **8.** | One hand washes | **h)** | sweat. |
| **9.** | One swallow does | **i)** | the other. |
| **10.** | Opportunity | **j)** | the world go round. |

| | | | |
|---|---|---|---|
| **11.** | Opposites | **a)** | and he is bound to appear. |
| **12.** | Poverty is | **b)** | attract. |
| **13.** | Practice makes | **c)** | but silence is golden. |
| **14.** | Revenge is | **d)** | catches the worm. |
| **15.** | Speak of the devil, | **e)** | far from the tree. |
| **16.** | Speech is silver | **f)** | no sin. |
| **17.** | Strike while | **g)** | perfect. |
| **18.** | The apple never falls | **h)** | sweet. |
| **19.** | The bigger they are, | **i)** | the harder they fall. |
| **20.** | The early bird | **j)** | the iron is hot. |

## TEST 87 Finden Sie die logische Entsprechung.

burn ~~Brazil~~ cook fish freeze fruit fun hot Hungary melody modern monk month sad see solid tablecloth war

1. Volga : Russia = Amazon : Brazil
2. walking stick : to walk = spectacles : to ____________
3. wall : wall paper = table : ____________
4. waltz : rock music : old-fashioned : ____________
5. warm : to boil = cold : to ____________
6. Warsaw : Poland = Budapest : ____________
7. washing machine : to wash = stove : to ____________
8. water : fire = to drown : to ____________
9. water : liquid = ice : ____________
10. Wednesday : day = July : ____________
11. wheat : cereal = peach : ____________
12. white : black = happy : ____________
13. wind : storm = conflict : ____________
14. wings : birds = fins : ____________
15. winter : cold = summer : ____________
16. woman : man = nun : ____________
17. word : sentence = note : ____________
18. work : serious = games : ____________

**Setzen Sie ein.**



accept cake chicken condition enough Good know learn letters luggage more ~~Make~~ old Open pace probably right sold Sorry tomorrow

1. Mach das Beste aus dieser Gelegenheit. > Make the most of this opportunity.
2. wahrscheinlich kommt er heute nicht > he will ____________ not come today
3. Tut mir leid, falsch verbunden! > ________, wrong number!
4. man kann nie wissen > you never ________
5. Danke, das genügt. > That's __________, thank you.
6. Ich möchte ein Brötchen mit Hähnchenfleisch. > I'd like a __________ roll.
7. rechts fahren > to drive on the ________
8. seine helle Freude haben an > to be ________ than delighted at
9. Deutsch lernen > to ________ German
10. Öffnen Sie dieses Paket. > ________ this package.
11. Er hat sein Auto verkauft. > He ________ his car.
12. Sie ist achtzehn Jahre alt. > She is eighteen years ________.
13. Ein Stück Kuchen, bitte. > I'd like a piece of ________, please.
14. Bis morgen! > See you ____________!
15. mit schnellen Schritten > at a brisk ________
16. Akzeptieren Sie eine Kreditkarte? > Do you __________ credit cards?
17. unter einer Bedingung > on one ______________
18. Holen Sie bitte mein Gepäck ab. > Please collect my __________.
19. Ist Post für mich da? > Are there any ____________ for me?
20. Guten Abend! > ________ evening!

**TEST 89** **Finden Sie waagerecht oder senkrecht 29 europäische Länder.**

| | | | | | | | | | | | | | | | |
|---|---|---|---|---|---|---|---|---|---|---|---|---|---|---|---|
| T | I | G | F | N | C | N | D | I | Q | R | G | B | F | A | L |
| U | R | R | R | O | Y | S | E | C | B | X | E | U | Z | L | U |
| R | E | E | A | R | P | W | N | E | Z | J | R | **Y** | H | B | S |
| K | L | E | N | W | R | I | M | L | S | Q | M | **U** | G | A | D |
| E | A | C | C | A | U | T | A | A | L | B | A | **G** | L | N | P |
| Y | N | E | E | Y | S | Z | R | N | O | U | N | **O** | U | I | O |
| R | D | H | A | R | G | E | K | D | V | L | Y | **S** | X | A | R |
| S | W | E | D | E | N | R | J | X | A | G | S | **L** | E | Q | T |
| P | O | L | A | N | D | L | W | H | K | A | P | **A** | M | K | U |
| A | U | S | T | R | I | A | K | J | I | R | A | **V** | B | B | G |
| C | S | L | O | V | E | N | I | A | A | I | I | **I** | O | E | A |
| B | O | S | N | I | A | D | B | J | Z | A | N | **A** | U | L | L |
| L | K | N | E | T | H | E | R | L | A | N | D | S | R | G | Z |
| Z | R | I | H | U | N | G | A | R | Y | L | M | P | G | I | D |
| C | R | O | A | T | I | A | R | O | M | A | N | I | A | U | X |
| R | U | S | S | I | A | F | I | N | L | A | N | D | X | M | S |

**Finden Sie Wortpaare mit gegenteiliger Bedeutung.** **TEST 90**

black boring cheap dead far fast few hard healthy high ~~lazy~~ left light long married small southern stupid thin ugly

1. hardworking - lazy
2. large / big - ____________
3. fat - ____________
4. slow - ____________
5. beautiful - ____________
6. near - ____________
7. dark - ____________
8. expensive - ____________
9. intelligent - ____________
10. white - ____________
11. soft - ____________
12. many - ____________
13. alive - ____________
14. exciting - ____________
15. low - ____________
16. northern - ____________
17. short - ____________
18. ill - ____________
19. single - ____________
20. right - ____________

## TEST 91 Setzen Sie ein.

at bill breath ~~business~~ coat created cross deserved forbidden holiday How into mood pieces problem speak television there Turn well

1. das ist nicht deine Sache > that's none of your business
2. Was kostet das Buch? > ______ much is this book?
3. ebenso gut wie > as ________ as
4. ich habe ihn zu Hause angetroffen > I found him ______ home
5. der Mantel passt mir > the ________ fits me
6. die Straße überqueren / über die Straße gehen > to __________ the street
7. ein schwieriger Punkt > a knotty ______________
8. eine gerechte Strafe > a well-________________ punishment
9. Wir haben 100 Stück auf Lager. > We have 100 _________ in stock.
10. fließend sprechen > to __________ fluently
11. im Fernsehen sehen > to see on ____________________
12. in Stücke schneiden > to cut ________ pieces
13. er hat ein Meisterwerk geschaffen > he has __________ a masterpiece
14. es donnert > __________ is thunder
15. es ist verboten zu halten > it is ____________ to stop
16. Stell das Radio an! > ________ on the radio!
17. Könnten wir bitte die Rechnung haben? > Could we have the ___________, please?
18. auf Urlaub / im Urlaub > on ______________ / on vacation
19. außer Atem > out of ____________
20. guter Laune sein / guten Mutes sein / guter Stimmung sein > to be in a good ________

**Setzen Sie die Sätze in die richtige Reihenfolge.**



- ◯ A spark in the machine had caused an explosion which had burnt down the whole apartment.
- (1) A young man in a French town claimed he was better at household chores than his wife.
- ◯ He had to take care of things on his own.
- ◯ He learnt to iron, cook, clean and wash.
- ◯ He remembered that his mother had told him that gasoline cleans exceptionally well.
- ◯ One day he wanted to get rid of a particularly problematic stain on his clothes.
- ◯ So she left him.
- ◯ So, he poured gasoline instead of washing powder into the washing machine.
- ◯ The stain was also gone.
- ◯ Then he went shopping.
- ◯ When he returned, his apartment had disappeared.

**TEST 93** Schreiben Sie den Text mit Leerzeichen und Satzzeichen.

THELADYWHOHADTHEMAXIMUMNUMBEROFCHILDRENINGERMA
NYLIVEDABOUT500YEARSAGOHERTOMBSTONESTATESTHATS
HEGAVEBIRTHTO38BOYSAND15GIRLSATOTALOF53BABIESTHIS
ISNOTAHIGHNUMBERWHENCOMPAREDTOARUSSIANFARMER'SWIF
EWHOISSUPPOSEDTOHAVEHAD69CHILDRENALMOSTALLOFWHOMW
EREBORNASQUADRUPLETSTRIPLETSORTWINSITISNOTKNOWN
HOWMANYOFTHEMSURVIVED

**Setzen Sie ein.**

allowed an anybody anything as cheque customers Christmas damaged ~~directory~~ help much order Right seventy skin sorry tomorrow working

1. Haben Sie ein Telefonbuch? > Have you got a telephone directory?
2. Darf man Hunde mitbringen? > Are dogs ____________?
3. Ich brauche einen Dolmetscher, der mir hilft. > I need ____ interpreter to help me.
4. Ich möchte einen Reisescheck einlösen. > I'd like to cash a traveller's _________.
5. Die meisten Kunden sind ältere Leute. > Most of the _________ are elderly people.
6. Mein Wagen wurde beschädigt. > My car has been _________.
7. er ist nur Haut und Knochen > he is nothing but _______ and bones
8. Richtig! / Das stimmt! > _________! / Quite so!
9. Die Heizung funktioniert nicht. > The heating isn't _____ properly.
10. wie gewöhnlich / wie sonst > ____ usual
11. siebzig Meter hoch > ____________ metres high
12. viel weniger > _______ less
13. Bitte deinen Papa um Hilfe. > Ask your Dad for _______.
14. Am ... habe ich bei Ihnen eine Bestellung aufgegeben. > On ... I placed an _________ with you.
15. Entschuldigen Sie! / Entschuldigung! > I beg your pardon! / (I am) _________!
16. morgen ist Sonntag > ______________ is Sunday
17. irgend etwas > something / ______________
18. Fröhliche Weihnachten! > Merry _______________!
19. Ist jemand hier? > Is ____________ there?

## TEST 95 Finden Sie die logische Entsprechung.

art beverage blue calculate cars chemical colour economic fish floor hate intelligence paint ~~participants~~ penguin people roof Romania speech Slovakia

1. organisation : members = conference : participants
2. Oslo : Norway = Bucharest : ____________________
3. oval : shape = pink : ____________________
4. parents : children = government : ____________________
5. pastor : sermon = politician : ____________________
6. pasture : green = water : ____________________
7. peace : war = love : ____________________
8. pen : to write = calculator : to ____________________
9. north pole : south pole = polar bear : ____________________
10. pepper : spice = mineral water : ____________________
11. person : umbrella = house : ____________________
12. photo : to photograph = painting : to ____________________
13. Physics : physical = Chemistry : ____________________
14. wallpaper : wall = carpet : ____________________
15. pigeon : bird = trout : ____________________
16. polite : politeness = intelligent : ____________________
17. politician : politics = artist : ____________________
18. politics : political = economy : ____________________
19. port : ships = car park : ____________________
20. Prague : Czech Republic = Bratislava : ____________________

**Finden Sie waagerecht oder senkrecht 27 Sportarten.**



| | | | | | | | | | | | | | | | |
|---|---|---|---|---|---|---|---|---|---|---|---|---|---|---|---|
| F | P | K | A | L | S | W | I | M | M | I | N | G | E | G | Z |
| O | H | O | C | K | E | Y | L | M | S | A | I | L | I | N | G |
| O | K | B | S | H | S | K | A | T | I | N | G | S | J | G | V |
| T | F | O | Y | R | I | D | I | N | G | B | Q | D | W | L | R |
| B | E | X | V | C | H | E | S | S | C | T | E | N | N | I | S |
| A | N | I | **W** | **I** | **N** | **D** | **S** | **U** | **R** | **F** | **I** | **N** | **G** | D | P |
| L | C | N | S | H | B | S | J | V | Z | H | D | M | C | I | V |
| L | I | G | H | A | A | K | W | R | Q | U | R | O | F | N | W |
| B | N | D | O | N | D | I | S | O | S | R | Z | S | G | G | R |
| O | G | V | O | D | M | I | A | W | H | D | H | N | S | C | E |
| W | K | P | T | B | I | N | B | I | L | L | I | A | R | D | S |
| L | A | O | I | A | N | G | Z | N | D | I | V | I | N | G | T |
| I | R | L | N | L | T | Q | Y | G | I | N | E | E | Z | N | L |
| N | A | O | G | L | O | J | U | D | O | G | A | D | G | W | I |
| G | T | F | Z | L | N | D | G | O | L | F | L | Q | D | M | N |
| O | E | B | C | V | O | L | L | E | Y | B | A | L | L | X | G |

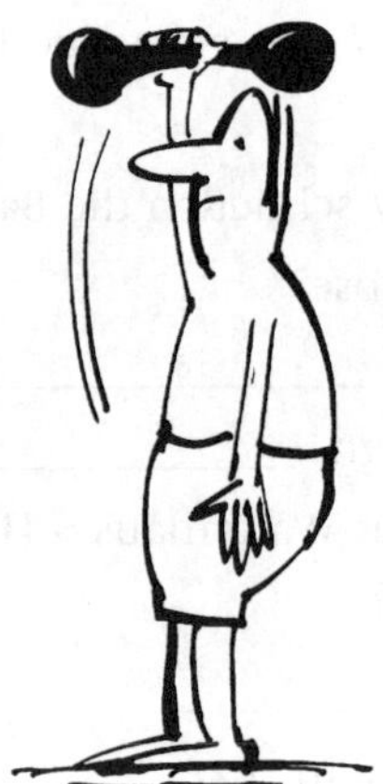

## TEST 97 Setzen Sie ein.

banks bear breakdown can clock country discussion first has in languages night ~~nine~~ piece pretending roll store think way without

1. halb zehn > half past nine
2. darüber lässt sich streiten > that's open to ______________
3. das versteht sich von selbst > that goes ____________ saying
4. ich habe kein Interesse daran > I am not interested ______ it
5. der, die, das erste > the _________
6. Wie alt schätzt du ihn? > How old do you _________ he is?
7. die ganze Nacht > all _________
8. Sie müssen in drei Monaten wieder ausreisen. > You must leave the ____________ again in three months.
9. ein Stück Holz > a _________ of wood
10. eine Panne haben > to have a ________________
11. einen Film entwickeln > to develop a _______ of film
12. Wir können Ihnen einen Nachlass von 10% anbieten. > We _____ give you a discount of 10%.
13. alles bleibt beim Alten > nothing _____ changed
14. im Gedächtnis behalten / sich etwas merken / etwas behalten > to _______ in mind
15. Um wieviel Uhr öffnen / schließen die Banken? > What time do the _________ open / close?
16. er tut nur so > he is just __________________
17. fremde Sprachen > foreign ________________
18. Harrods ist ein bekanntes Warenhaus > Harrods is a famous department _________
19. es ist vier Uhr > it is 4 o'_________
20. auf diese Art und Weise > in that _____

**Was passt zusammen?**
**Bilden Sie Sprichwörter oder Redensarten.**



| | | | |
|---|---|---|---|
| **1.** | The exception | **a)** | always goes barefoot. |
| **2.** | The leopard cannot | **b)** | by its fruit. |
| **3.** | The love of money is | **c)** | change its spots. |
| **4.** | The road to hell is paved | **d)** | is human. |
| **5.** | The shoemaker's son | **e)** | is money. |
| **6.** | The sun shines | **f)** | proves the rule. |
| **7.** | The tree is known | **g)** | the root of all evil. |
| **8.** | There are two sides | **h)** | to everything. |
| **9.** | Time | **i)** | upon all alike. |
| **10.** | To err | **j)** | with good intentions. |

| | | | |
|---|---|---|---|
| **11.** | Too many cooks | **a)** | cross to bear. |
| **12.** | We all have our | **b)** | do as the Romans do. |
| **13.** | Well begun | **c)** | is half done. |
| **14.** | When in Rome, | **d)** | spoil the broth. |
| **15.** | When the cat's away | **e)** | the forest for the trees. |
| **16.** | Where there is smoke | **f)** | the mice will play. |
| **17.** | Where there's a will | **g)** | there's a way. |
| **18.** | You can't see | **h)** | there's fire. |
| **19.** | You can't have | **i)** | without breaking eggs. |
| **20.** | You can't make an omelette | **j)** | your cake and eat it. |

**TEST 99** Was macht man mit dem Mund?
Finden Sie waagerecht oder senkrecht 18 Verben.

| | | | | | | | | | | | | |
|---|---|---|---|---|---|---|---|---|---|---|---|---|
| s | b | d | s | g | k | b | o | j | s | c | d | l |
| m | l | c | n | b | z | x | y | z | p | m | o | t |
| i | o | v | o | g | s | v | f | k | e | i | t | h |
| l | w | j | r | m | i | a | n | c | a | l | l | j |
| e | a | t | e | w | b | d | d | u | k | c | x | g |
| l | **b** | **e** | **l** | **l** | **o** | **w** | c | z | s | i | n | g |
| y | s | d | x | t | l | a | u | g | h | u | n | v |
| p | p | f | o | d | s | y | y | a | w | n | v | h |
| h | i | d | c | o | u | g | h | s | u | c | k | l |
| n | t | e | k | i | s | s | c | f | j | j | b | k |
| g | z | v | d | r | i | n | k | n | y | u | i | x |
| o | y | x | s | w | h | i | s | p | e | r | t | t |
| k | c | h | e | w | c | x | k | y | y | E | e | f |

**Setzen Sie ein.**

blocked boring brother comfortable connected directions find ~~fish~~ insurance leg look matters receipt soon tell temper took touch translation wants

1. Haben Sie gekochtes Huhn oder gekochten Fisch? > Is there any boiled chicken or boiled fish?
2. nach allen Seiten > in all ___________
3. Das Waschbecken ist verstopft. > The wash-basin is ___________.
4. Ich habe ein Taxi vom Flughafen genommen. > I _______ a taxi from the airport.
5. Sie müssen den Unfall Ihrer Versicherungsgesellschaft melden. > You must report the accident to your _________ company.
6. schlecht aussehen > to _______ ill
7. je mehr man hat, desto mehr man will > the more one has, the more one _________
8. Geben Sie mir eine Quittung? > May I have a ___________?
9. mein jüngerer Bruder > my younger ___________
10. sich das Bein brechen > to break one's _____
11. Die Reise war sehr bequem. > The journey was very _________.
12. Bitte nicht berühren! > Do not _________!
13. Mittel und Wege finden > to _______ ways and means
14. in Verbindung stehen mit > to be ___________ with
15. so steht die Sache > that's how ___________ stand
16. Können Sie mir sagen, wo das Konsulat ist? > Can you _______ me where the consulate is?
17. Dieser Film ist langweilig. > This movie is ___________ .
18. Er machte die russisch-französische Übersetzung. > He did the Russian to French ___________.
19. wütend werden > to lose one's ___________
20. Auf Wiedersehen! / Bis bald! > Good-bye!/ So long!/ See you _____!

# LÖSUNGEN

**TEST 1:**

**1.** cross **2.** aloud **3.** pick **4.** work **5.** fond **6.** different **7.** application **8.** haircut **9.** special **10.** travel **11.** map **12.** at **13.** pieces **14.** German **15.** possible **16.** send **17.** only **18.** duty **19.** be **20.** result

**TEST 2:**

| | | | | | |
|---|---|---|---|---|---|
| **1.** | flower | vase | **I.** | bicycle | bell |
| **2.** | car | boot / trunk | **II.** | theatre | stage |
| **3.** | train | ticket | **III.** | pub | beer |
| **4.** | coffee | sugar | **IV.** | circus | clown |
| **5.** | pot | lid | **V.** | jacket | leather |

| | | | | | |
|---|---|---|---|---|---|
| **a)** | soup | spoon | **A)** | zoo | animals |
| **b)** | fever | thermometer | **B)** | computer | printer |
| **c)** | stairs | banisters | **C)** | sky | star |
| **d)** | sausage | mustard | **D)** | disco | music |
| **e)** | snow | ski lift | **E)** | luggage | suitcase |

**TEST 3:**

| | | | |
|---|---|---|---|
| **1.** | interesting - boring | **11.** | fresh - stale |
| **2.** | tall - short | **12.** | late - early |
| **3.** | rich - poor | **13.** | wet - dry |
| **4.** | sad - happy | **14.** | old - young |
| **5.** | new - old | **15.** | full - empty |
| **6.** | smooth - rough | **16.** | right - wrong |
| **7.** | sharp - blunt | **17.** | transparent - opaque |
| **8.** | clean - dirty | **18.** | always - never |
| **9.** | up - down | **19.** | heavy - light |
| **10.** | top - bottom | **20.** | polite - rude |

**TEST 4:**

**1.** piece **2.** money **3.** quite **4.** listening **5.** understand **6.** Keep **7.** windshield **8.** test **9.** upset **10.** town **11.** receipt **12.** taste **13.** beginning **14.** next **15.** Can **16.** Follow **17.** recommended **18.** Turn **19.** tree

**TEST 5:**

| | | | |
|---|---|---|---|
| **1.** | church | **11.** | French |
| **2.** | captain | **12.** | baker |
| **3.** | to eat | **13.** | milk |
| **4.** | river | **14.** | death |
| **5.** | to forbid | **15.** | future |
| **6.** | Bulgaria | **16.** | continent |
| **7.** | south | **17.** | restaurant |
| **8.** | earth | **18.** | dwarf |
| **9.** | ocean | **19.** | mouth |
| **10.** | Arabic | **20.** | to listen |

**TEST 6:**

black blue brown grey green orange pink purple red white yellow

**TEST 7:**

**1.** scenery **2.** anything **3.** equals **4.** headache **5.** right **6.** Sunday **7.** cracked **8.** else **9.** educated **10.** play **11.** mistake **12.** by **13.** cinema **14.** touch **15.** head **16.** speaks **17.** times **18.** yesterday **19.** fault **20.** to

**TEST 8:**

| | | | | | |
|---|---|---|---|---|---|
| **1.** | wall | brick | **I.** | Berlin | city |
| **2.** | hand | finger | **II.** | weather | snow |
| **3.** | racket | tennis ball | **III.** | night | darkness |
| **4.** | lamp | bulb | **IV.** | thirst | beer |
| **5.** | banana | peel | **V.** | bottle | cork |

| | | | | | |
|---|---|---|---|---|---|
| **a.** | suit | tie | **A.** | tree | trunk |
| **b.** | computer | mouse | **B.** | television | programme |
| **c.** | football | goal | **C.** | bread | slice |
| **d.** | book | page | **D.** | leg | foot |
| **e.** | coffee | sugar | **E.** | grammar | rules |

**TEST 9:**

1. hard
2. cloud
3. happy
4. apples
5. Benelux
6. service
7. spinach
8. throat
9. weather
10. street
11. tree
12. architect
13. petrol
14. Zurich
15. hill
16. visit
17. handwriting
18. Brazil
19. fork
20. computer

**TEST 10:**

**1.** accident **2.** laughing **3.** mountain **4.** do **5.** if **6.** electrician **7.** later **8.** tooth **9.** varies **10.** will **11.** accept **12.** floor **13.** what **14.** beer **15.** water **16.** as **17.** French **18.** collect **19.** enquiry **20.** dog

**TEST 11:**

1. A barking dog never bites.
2. A bird in the hand is worth two in the bush.
3. A friend in need is a friend indeed.
4. A liar is not believed even when he speaks the truth.
5. A single stroke won't fell an oak.
6. Actions speak louder than words.
7. All's fair in love and war.
8. All roads lead to Rome.
9. All that glitters is not gold.
10. All things must come to an end.
11. All's well that ends well.
12. An eye for an eye, a tooth for a tooth.
13. A man's home is his castle.
14. You've made your bed, now lie in it.
15. Better late than never.
16. Big fish eat little fish.
17. Brevity is the soul of wit.
18. Caution is the mother of wisdom.
19. Cold hands, warm heart.
20. Dead men tell no tales.

**TEST 12:**

**1.** spend **2.** obliged **3.** wine **4.** wake **5.** post **6.** second **7.** dishes **8.** read **9.** enter **10.** such **11.** smoke **12.** benefit **13.** receipt **14.** this **15.** down **16.** thinking **17.** only **18.** succeeded **19.** late **20.** love

**TEST 13:**

| | | | | | | | | | | | | | | |
|---|---|---|---|---|---|---|---|---|---|---|---|---|---|---|
| 1 S | P | 2 E | A | 3 K | | 4 S | 5 T | 6 E | A | M | 7 B | O | A | 8 T |
| E | | X | | N | | 9 T | O | Y | | | R | | | H |
| A | | 10 P | H | O | N | E | | 11 E | A | 12 R | A | 13 C | H | E |
| 14 S | E | E | | C | | W | | | | E | | I | | I |
| O | | 15 C | A | K | E | | 16 S | 17 T | R | A | N | G | E | R |
| N | | T | | I | | 18 O | | A | | D | | A | | |
| 19 I | 20 T | S | | 21 N | A | P | 22 K | I | N | | 23 T | R | 24 E | 25 E |
| 26 N | O | | | G | | 27 E | E | L | | 28 M | | | 29 A | M |
| 30 G | E | 31 T | S | | 32 A | N | Y | O | N | E | | 33 A | R | E |
| | | I | | 34 I | | E | | R | | D | | N | | R |
| 35 L | E | M | O | N | A | D | E | | 36 K | I | L | O | | G |
| I | | E | | T | | | | 37 T | | C | | 38 T | I | E |
| 39 L | E | S | 40 S | O | N | 41 S | | 42 I | R | I | S | H | | N |
| A | | | E | | | 43 A | 44 I | R | | N | | E | | C |
| 45 C | I | G | A | R | E | T | T | E | | 46 E | A | R | L | Y |

**TEST 14:**

| | | | | | | | | | | | |
|---|---|---|---|---|---|---|---|---|---|---|---|
| | | R | **H** | I | N | O | C | E | R | O | S |
| | | G | **I** | R | A | F | F | E | | | |
| | | | **P** | E | N | G | U | I | N | | |
| E | L | E | **P** | H | A | N | T | | | | |
| | | F | **O** | X | | | | | | | |
| L | E | O | **P** | A | R | D | | | | | |
| | | W | **O** | L | F | | | | | | |
| | | | **T** | I | G | E | R | | | | |
| | B | E | **A** | R | | | | | | | |
| | C | A | **M** | E | L | | | | | | |
| | | T | **U** | R | T | L | E | | | | |
| | | | **S** | N | A | K | E | | | | |

**TEST 15:**

**1.** glasses **2.** racket **3.** fear **4.** Mexicans **5.** Greece **6.** Christianity **7.** rooms **8.** station **9.** expensive **10.** bell **11.** engine **12.** leg **13.** floor **14.** restaurant **15.** slow **16.** box **17.** Koran **18.** study **19.** liver **20.** healthy

**TEST 16:**

**1.** so **2.** vegetables **3.** never **4.** stay **5.** morning **6.** meat **7.** Leave **8.** people **9.** change **10.** cut **11.** fastest **12.** age **13.** Catholic **14.** running **15.** placed **16.** used **17.** finish **18.** been **19.** books **20.** only

**TEST 17:**

1. Do not throw pearls before swine.
2. Don't count your chickens before they hatch.
3. Easy come, easy go.
4. Faith will move mountains.
5. First come, first served.
6. Fish and wine go together.
7. Four eyes see more than two.
8. God helps those who help themselves.
9. He who laughs last, laughs longest.
10. Honey catches more flies than vinegar.
11. Honour to whom honour is due.
12. If you grease well, you speed well.
13. In the country of the blind, the one-eyed man is king.
14. It is better to give than to receive.
15. Knowledge is power.
16. Lies have short legs.
17. Little thieves are hanged, but great ones escape.
18. Love is blind.
19. Lucky at cards, unlucky in love.
20. Man proposes, God disposes.

**TEST 18:**

1. envelope
2. breathe
3. leather
4. dry
5. Egypt
6. beggar
7. rubber
8. steal
9. drops
10. Austria
11. seats
12. bird
13. French
14. dangerous
15. rain
16. Christmas
17. baker
18. truth
19. notes
20. frame

**TEST 19:**

**1.** comfort **2.** lose **3.** trust **4.** Sit **5.** milk **6.** exchange **7.** Look **8.** fits **9.** sign **10.** pass **11.** profession **12.** electricity **13.** children **14.** name **15.** than **16.** today **17.** car **18.** table **19.** feel **20.** learn

**TEST 20:**

| | |
|---|---|
| **1.** chin | beard |
| **2.** church | pope |
| **3.** lightning | thunder |
| **4.** wine | glass |
| **5.** car | petrol |

| | |
|---|---|
| **I.** tree | wood |
| **II.** face | nose |
| **III.** question | answer |
| **IV.** judge | verdict |
| **V.** cause | effect |

| | |
|---|---|
| **a.** shirt | collar |
| **b.** sports | Olympics |
| **c.** sky | cloud |
| **d.** music | notes |
| **e.** word | letters |

| | |
|---|---|
| **A.** heater | warmth |
| **B.** plant | leaf |
| **C.** money | wallet |
| **D.** apartment | rent |
| **E.** parties | elections |

**TEST 21:**

**1.** fingernail **2.** shoulder **3.** stomach **4.** eyebrow **5.** tongue **6.** throat **7.** finger **8.** breast **9.** tooth **10.** thumb **11.** mouth **12.** cheek **13.** bosom **14.** beard **15.** skin **16.** nose **17.** neck **18.** knee **19.** head **20.** hand **21.** hair **22.** face **23.** chin **24.** bone

**TEST 22:**

**1.** here **2.** or **3.** turn **4.** care **5.** whenever **6.** less **7.** manners **8.** yesterday **9.** tell **10.** about **11.** were **12.** voice **13.** please **14.** radio **15.** hand **16.** morning **17.** glad **18.** about **19.** home **20.** long

**TEST 23:**

1. to give - to take
2. to accept - to refuse
3. to freeze - to melt
4. to push - to pull
5. to approve - to disapprove
6. to lock - to unlock
7. to succeed - to fail
8. to appear - to disappear
9. to lend - to borrow
10. to ascend - to descend
11. to search - to find
12. to trust - to distrust
13. to break - to fix
14. to halve - to double
15. to forget - to remember
16. to agree - to disagree
17. to tie - to untie
18. to behave - to misbehave
19. to throw - to catch
20. to follow - to lead

**TEST 24:**

| | | | | | | | | | | | | | | | | |
|---|---|---|---|---|---|---|---|---|---|---|---|---|---|---|---|---|
| | | | | | | | | | | The | | | | | | |
| | | | | | | S | P | A | I | **N** | | | | | | |
| | | | | | | | | S | W | **E** | D | E | N | | | |
| | | | | | | | | | | **T** | U | R | K | E | Y | |
| | | | | | | | | | | **H** | U | N | G | A | R | Y |
| | | | | | | S | L | O | V | **E** | N | I | A | | | |
| | | | | | | | | | | **R** | U | S | S | I | A | |
| | | | | | | | | | S | **L** | O | V | A | K | I | A |
| | | | | P | O | R | T | U | G | **A** | L | | | | | |
| | | | | | | R | O | M | A | **N** | I | A | | | | |
| S | W | I | T | Z | E | R | L | A | N | **D** | | | | | | |
| | | | | | | Y | U | G | O | **S** | L | A | V | I | A | |

**TEST 25:**

**1.** plastic **2.** cook **3.** stroke **4.** matter **5.** thing **6.** glasses **7.** hands **8.** run **9.** Summer **10.** history **11.** slow **12.** temperature **13.** taste **14.** day **15.** Where **16.** raining **17.** razor **18.** May **19.** case **20.** sharp

**TEST 26:**

**1.** stage
**2.** conductor
**3.** dead
**4.** temperature
**5.** uniform
**6.** to roar
**7.** white
**8.** glass
**9.** heater
**10.** to write
**11.** referee
**12.** police
**13.** red
**14.** cutlery
**15.** glass
**16.** hard
**17.** person
**18.** peace
**19.** darkness
**20.** Indonesia

**TEST 27:**

| | | | | | | | | | | | | | | |
|---|---|---|---|---|---|---|---|---|---|---|---|---|---|---|
| 1 P | A | 2 I | N | 3 T | E | 4 D | | 5 D | | 6 T | R | 7 I | E | D |
| R | | N | | U | | I | | E | | R | | R | | |
| 8 O | F | F | E | R | | 9 F | A | C | T | O | R | I | E | 10 S |
| U | | L | | K | | F | | K | | U | | S | | W |
| 11 D | I | A | B | E | T | I | C | | 12 A | S | T | H | M | A |
| | | T | | Y | | C | | 13 A | | E | | | | L |
| 14 S | H | I | P | | 15 S | U | 16 P | P | E | R | | 17 A | L | L |
| E | | O | | 18 R | | 19 L | I | P | | S | | E | | O |
| 20 V | A | N | | 21 E | N | T | E | R | S | | 22 B | R | E | W |
| E | | | | M | | Y | | O | | 23 A | | O | | |
| 24 N | E | 25 P | H | E | W | | 26 B | A | G | P | I | P | E | 27 S |
| T | | R | | M | | 28 M | | C | | P | | L | | W |
| 29 H | A | I | R | B | R | U | S | H | | 30 L | E | A | V | E |
| | | N | | E | | C | | E | | E | | N | | E |
| 31 E | N | T | E | R | | H | | 32 D | E | S | S | E | R | T |

**TEST 28:**

**1.** reason **2.** enough **3.** would **4.** drive **5.** younger **6.** do **7.** with **8.** health **9.** well **10.** times **11.** quarter **12.** walk **13.** hardly **14.** turn **15.** rule **16.** touch **17.** tomorrow **18.** not **19.** there **20.** better

**TEST 29:**

**1.** autumn / fall (am.) **2.** July **3.** seven **4.** Thursday **5.** stars **6.** February **7.** four **8.** backward **9.** Wednesday **10.** third **11.** today **12.** never **13.** South **14.** future **15.** above

**TEST 30:**

| | | | | | | | | | | | | | | |
|---|---|---|---|---|---|---|---|---|---|---|---|---|---|---|
| 1 C | U | 2 P | | 3 B | R | 4 I | E | 5 F | | 6 A | 7 C | T | 8 O | R |
| A | | O | | R | | N | | L | | | A | | U | |
| 9 R | H | I | N | E | | 10 T | R | A | N | 11 S | P | 12 O | R | T |
| | | S | | A | | R | | T | | H | | W | | |
| 13 B | O | O | K | S | H | O | P | | 14 P | R | I | E | S | 15 T |
| | | N | | T | | D | | 16 C | | I | | | | H |
| 17 S | U | I | T | | 18 M | U | 19 S | E | U | M | | 20 A | G | E |
| L | | N | | 21 O | | 22 C | A | N | | P | | M | | R |
| 23 E | G | G | | 24 P | R | E | T | T | Y | | 25 A | B | L | E |
| E | | | | E | | D | | I | | 26 B | | U | | |
| 27 P | O | 28 L | A | N | D | | 29 U | M | B | R | E | L | L | A |
| | | I | | E | | 30 H | | E | | A | | A | | |
| 31 I | 32 M | P | 33 O | R | T | A | N | T | | 34 N | I | N | T | 35 H |
| | E | | F | | | V | | R | | D | | C | | E |
| 36 K | N | I | F | E | | 37 E | V | E | R | Y | | 38 E | A | R |

**TEST 31:**

**1.** salt **2.** Make **3.** coming **4.** damage **5.** performance **6.** drink **7.** car **8.** machine **9.** hospital **10.** charge **11.** No **12.** sea **13.** Noon **14.** shoes **15.** Good **16.** door **17.** dog **18.** God **19.** surprise **20.** too

**TEST 32:**

1. crocodile
2. day
3. fleet
4. head
5. twelve
6. shampoo
7. deep
8. to hiss
9. summer
10. to lie
11. boss
12. water
13. verse
14. fork
15. oil
16. Dutch
17. beautiful
18. to drink
19. to reap
20. round

**TEST 33:**

A man has a sausage stand directly opposite a bank. An old friend comes and asks him: „Can you lend me some money?". „I'm sorry, I can't!" - „And why not?" - „Because I have a contract with the bank!" - „What kind of a contract?" - „I don't lend any money and they don't sell any sausages!"

**TEST 34:**

**1.** south **2.** nowhere **3.** back **4.** going **5.** watch **6.** something **7.** coat **8.** cross **9.** people **10.** bread **11.** question **12.** carry **13.** same **14.** advance **15.** fact **16.** age **17.** until **18.** need **19.** something **20.** mistake

**TEST 35:**

**1.** Danish
**2.** water
**3.** plant
**4.** mew
**5.** to swim
**6.** dinner
**7.** small
**8.** nose
**9.** salary
**10.** republic
**11.** season
**12.** architecture
**13.** deaf
**14.** to hear
**15.** cold
**16.** nearness
**17.** thin
**18.** princess

**TEST 36:**

**1.** direct - indirect
**2.** perfect - imperfect
**3.** loose - tight
**4.** together - separate
**5.** yesterday - tomorrow
**6.** flexible - inflexible
**7.** liquid - solid
**8.** now - later
**9.** offensive - defensive
**10.** noisy - quiet
**11.** scarce - abundant
**12.** arid - fertile
**13.** tolerant - intolerant
**14.** spicy - bland
**15.** arrogant - humble
**16.** plausible - implausible
**17.** shortsighted - longsighted
**18.** strong - weak

**TEST 37:**

**1.** any **2.** great **3.** Take **4.** would **5.** Welcome **6.** park **7.** another **8.** That **9.** skidded **10.** meet **11.** seriously **12.** over **13.** parking **14.** page **15.** ago **16.** nationality **17.** back **18.** road **19.** coffee **20.** hundreds

**TEST 38:**

1. arms
2. teeth
3. brain
4. lips
5. fist
6. nose
7. eyes
8. ears
9. tongue
10. heart
11. hands
12. finger
13. skin
14. hair
15. beard
16. neck
17. lungs
18. muscles
19. foot
20. legs

**TEST 39:**

| | | | | | | | | | | | | | | |
|---|---|---|---|---|---|---|---|---|---|---|---|---|---|---|
| 1 B | 2 A | 3 R | | 4 S | P | 5 O | R | 6 T | | 7 C | H | 8 E | A | 9 P |
| 10 A | G | E | | A | | U | | E | | U | | X | | R |
| 11 L | O | C | A | L | | 12 T | R | A | N | S | L | A | T | E |
| L | | E | | A | | | | M | | T | | C | | V |
| 13 S | E | P | A | R | A | 14 T | E | | 15 B | O | T | T | L | E |
| | | T | | Y | | O | | 16 N | | M | | | | N |
| 17 A | S | I | A | | 18 A | N | 19 Y | O | N | E | | 20 V | A | T |
| S | | O | | 21 A | | 22 G | E | T | | R | | A | | E |
| 23 P | E | N | | 24 C | O | U | S | I | N | | 25 I | C | E | D |
| A | | | | C | | E | | C | | 26 D | | C | | |
| 27 R | E | 28 P | A | I | R | | 29 C | E | R | A | M | I | C | 30 S |
| A | | R | | D | | 31 F | | | | N | | N | | P |
| 32 G | U | I | D | E | B | O | O | 33 K | | 34 G | R | A | 35 P | E |
| U | | Z | | N | | O | | E | | E | | 36 T | I | E |
| 37 S | W | E | E | T | | 38 D | R | Y | E | R | | 39 E | N | D |

**TEST 40:**

**1.** bad **2.** hungry **3.** ought **4.** weather **5.** aches **6.** understand **7.** rising **8.** rate **9.** funny **10.** pay **11.** coat **12.** Our **13.** height **14.** else **15.** on **16.** thirteen **17.** tomorrow **18.** nothing **19.** else **20.** side

**TEST 41:**

**1** Who **2** Where **3** Where **4** What **5** Who **6** Whom **7** How **8** Whose **9** Which **10** How **11** How **12** How **13** When **14** Why **15** Where **16** What **17** What **18** What **19** Since **20** Till

**TEST 42:**

1. sand
2. Greece
3. match
4. to stand
5. sky
6. fish
7. dolphin
8. Bavarian
9. December
10. goat
11. pencil
12. Europe
13. pot
14. friendly
15. spider
16. tomatoes
17. book
18. face
19. strong
20. hat

**TEST 43:**

**1.** declare **2.** latest **3.** give **4.** car **5.** night **6.** outdoors **7.** faithful **8.** television **9.** judge **10.** worry **11.** excludes **12.** other **13.** sick **14.** corner **15.** no **16.** by **17.** try **18.** need **19.** sauna **20.** present

**TEST 44:**

1. mayor
2. Spain
3. head
4. to sing
5. familiar
6. visitors
7. sweet
8. to believe
9. dry
10. Scandinavia
11. rocket
12. university
13. patient
14. to close
15. lazy
16. dog
17. divide
18. departure
19. defence
20. to finish

**TEST 45:**

1. stone
2. necklace
3. effect
4. barn
5. lungs
6. gun
7. to shoot
8. chocolate
9. animal
10. finger
11. licence
12. vodka
13. to slither
14. ashtray
15. kitchen
16. poor
17. city
18. brother
19. to explode
20. cheap

**TEST 46:**

**1.** trusted **2.** parking **3.** tune **4.** What **5.** doctor **6.** third **7.** Germany **8.** passed **9.** beautiful **10.** song **11.** task **12.** hour **13.** early **14.** garage **15.** Speak **16.** masterpiece **17.** in **18.** there **19.** stomach **20.** bicycle

**TEST 47:**

active
athletic
attractive
balanced
beautiful
brave
charming
cheerful
clean
elegant
exciting
fair
friendly
generous
hardworking
helpful
honest
humorous
intelligent
jolly
loving
neat
nice
optimistic
patient
polite
pretty
punctual
quiet
reliable
responsible
rich
sociable
strong
sympathetic
thin
tolerant
versatile

**TEST 48:**

| | | | | | | | | | | | | | | |
|---|---|---|---|---|---|---|---|---|---|---|---|---|---|---|
| 1 M | | 2 Y | E | 3 S | | 4 O | P | 5 E | R | 6 A | | 7 S | O | 8 N |
| O | | E | | 9 C | A | R | | X | | G | | H | | I |
| 10 P | A | S | T | A | | 11 C | H | A | I | R | | 12 I | C | E |
| E | | T | | L | | H | | C | | E | | F | | C |
| 13 D | Y | E | | 14 E | Y | E | | 15 T | 16 H | E | A | T | 17 R | E |
| | | R | | | | S | | | 18 A | M | | | U | |
| 19 I | N | D | I | 20 A | | 21 T | H | 22 E | S | E | | 23 A | N | 24 D |
| T | | A | | U | | R | | X | | N | | E | | I |
| 25 S | 26 A | Y | | 27 S | 28 T | A | M | P | | 29 T | I | R | E | D |
| | G | | | 30 T | O | | | L | | | | O | | |
| 31 C | O | 32 N | T | R | O | 33 L | | 34 A | R | 35 E | | 36 P | E | 37 A |
| O | | U | | A | | E | | I | | X | | L | | N |
| 38 A | I | R | | 39 L | E | A | R | N | | 40 T | R | A | I | N |
| S | | S | | I | | V | | 41 E | A | R | | N | | O |
| 42 T | H | E | | 43 A | H | E | A | D | | 44 A | G | E | | Y |

**TEST 49:**

**1.** forward **2.** remember **3.** would **4.** if **5.** change **6.** advice **7.** little **8.** broken **9.** break **10.** light **11.** less **12.** This **13.** thanks **14.** Good **15.** make **16.** your **17.** school **18.** soon **19.** some **20.** reserve

**TEST 50:**

1. vertical - horizontal
2. boisterous - calm
3. feminine - masculine
4. pessimistic - optimistic
5. microscopic - gigantic
6. famous - unknown
7. generous - stingy
8. colorful - drab
9. wild - tame
10. bare - covered
11. legal - illegal
12. temporary - permanent
13. physical - spiritual

**TEST 51:**

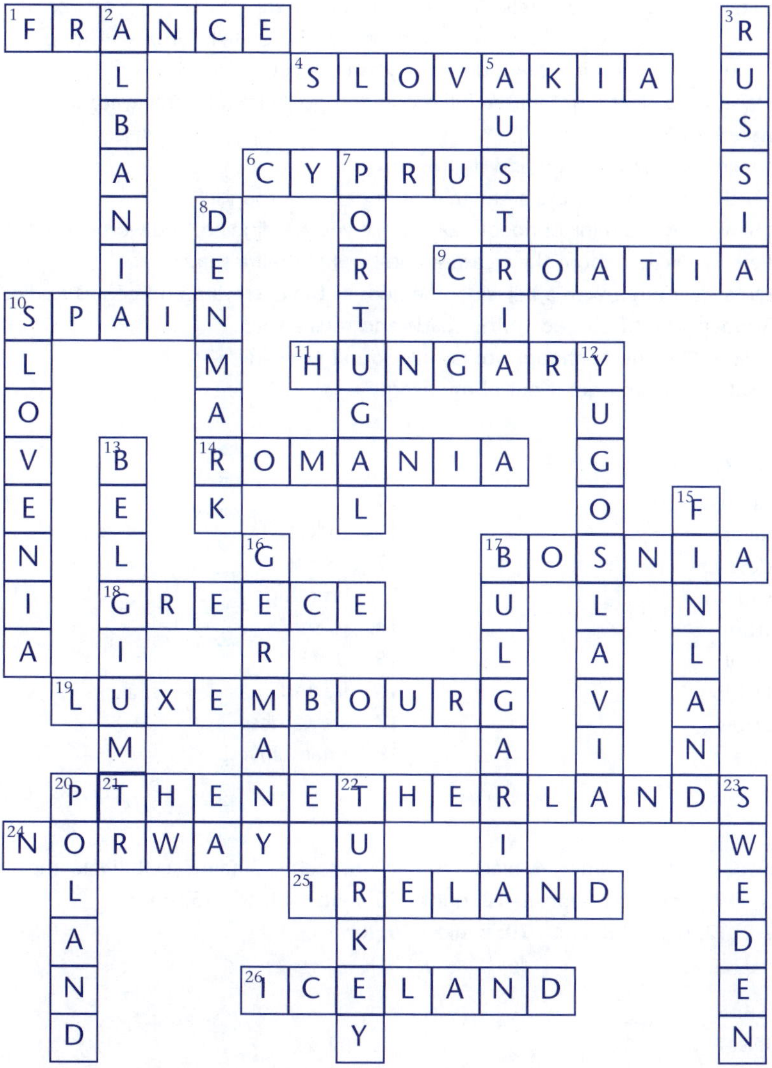


**TEST 52:**

**1.** cards **2.** enough **3.** want **4.** Have **5.** contact **6.** eggs **7.** left **8.** quarrel **9.** spoilt **10.** country **11.** once **12.** matches **13.** look **14.** beach **15.** outside **16.** out **17.** Shut **18.** repair **19.** doctor **20.** lose

**TEST 53:**

1. Peter goes to a fortune teller to ask about his future.
2. She looks into a crystal ball for a long time and then tells him:
3. "You will be very rich if you do exactly as I tell you."
4. "Wait for a clear night with a full moon and go to the old graveyard at midnight."
5. "Take a spade with you and dig for treasure."
6. "You'll find the treasure a few metres under the ground."
7. "Beware! If you think of noodle soup while you are digging, you won't find it."
8. Peter is excited about the treasure and buys himself a spade.
9. On a clear night with a full moon he goes to the graveyard and begins to dig.
10. Suddenly he throws down the spade and runs away:
11. "Damn! I've never thought of noodle soup in my life!"
12. „But now I can't get it out of my head!"

**TEST 54:**

1. disadvantage
2. failure
3. desert
4. sour
5. stop
6. alone
7. to blow
8. arrow
9. screw
10. shoe
11. to kiss
12. to cry
13. emotions
14. to see
15. devil
16. Ireland
17. stewardess
18. unemployed

**TEST 55:**

**1.** May **2.** cold **3.** same **4.** black **5.** two **6.** teeth **7.** faintest **8.** welcome **9.** soul **10.** these **11.** worse **12.** right **13.** fault **14.** of **15.** from **16.** else **17.** best **18.** first **19.** banks **20.** for

**TEST 56:**

1. false
2. true
3. true
4. true
5. true
6. false
7. true
8. true
9. true
10. true
11. false
12. false
13. true
14. false
15. true
16. false
17. true
18. false
19. true
20. false

**TEST 57:**

| | | | | | | | | | | | | | | |
|---|---|---|---|---|---|---|---|---|---|---|---|---|---|---|
| 1 M | U | 2 S | I | 3 C | | 4 R | E | 5 D | | 6 A | P | 7 P | L | 8 E |
| E | | O | | 9 I | C | E | | A | | I | | H | | N |
| 10 A | R | M | | N | | 11 M | O | T | O | R | | 12 O | L | D |
| N | | E | | E | | A | | E | | P | | T | | |
| 13 S | 14 A | W | | 15 M | O | R | E | | 16 A | L | M | O | N | 17 D |
| | 18 T | H | | A | | K | | 19 T | | A | | | | A |
| 20 H | E | E | L | | 21 W | A | S | H | I | N | G | 22 T | O | N |
| A | | R | | 23 E | | B | | R | | E | | R | | C |
| 24 T | H | E | M | S | E | L | V | E | S | | 25 R | A | 26 T | E |
| E | | | | C | | Y | | A | | 27 T | | 28 N | O | |
| 29 S | A | 30 N | D | A | L | | 31 S | T | A | R | | 32 S | E | 33 T |
| | | E | | L | | 34 W | | E | | A | | P | | H |
| 35 H | E | R | | 36 O | N | I | O | N | | V | | 37 O | N | E |
| O | | V | | P | | N | | 38 E | Y | E | | R | | R |
| 39 W | H | E | R | E | | 40 D | I | D | | 41 L | I | T | R | E |

**TEST 58:**

**1.** by **2.** lot **3.** vanilla **4.** pace **5.** holds **6.** shop **7.** recommended **8.** battery **9.** took **10.** his **11.** understands **12.** Open **13.** sample **14.** party **15.** taste **16.** limit **17.** luck **18.** or **19.** Cheer **20.** minute

**TEST 59:**

1. sailor
2. bedroom
3. air
4. pavement
5. permission
6. victory
7. to refuse
8. seal
9. oral
10. worthless
11. shell
12. pages
13. legs
14. work
15. guilt
16. to park
17. river
18. loud
19. country

**TEST 60:**

1. to win - to lose
2. to live - to die
3. to love - to hate
4. to buy - to sell
5. to depart - to arrive
6. to forbid - to allow
7. to attack - to defend
8. to come - to go
9. to command - to obey
10. to begin - to end
11. to question - to answer
12. to build - to destroy
13. to reward - to punish
14. to increase - to decrease
15. to send - to receive
16. to sow - to reap
17. to open - to close

**TEST 61:**

**1.** going **2.** anything **3.** swim **4.** hold **5.** nothing **6.** example **7.** knotty **8.** quite **9.** asleep **10.** other **11.** accompanied **12.** notebook **13.** day **14.** fall **15.** open **16.** place **17.** weather **18.** take **19.** come **20.** kind

**TEST 62:**

1. true
2. true
3. false
4. false
5. true
6. false
7. false
8. true
9. false
10. true
11. true
12. false
13. true
14. false
15. false
16. false
17. true
18. true
19. true
20. true

**TEST 63:**

**1.** serve **2.** When **3.** damaged **4.** weekend **5.** room **6.** light **7.** too **8.** cannot **9.** nice **10.** take **11.** late **12.** your **13.** Where **14.** Should **15.** wood **16.** away **17.** engine **18.** way **19.** does **20.** glass

**TEST 64:**

| | | | | | | | | | | | | | | |
|---|---|---|---|---|---|---|---|---|---|---|---|---|---|---|
| 1 C | O | 2 S | T | 3 S | | 4 T | 5 H | 6 A | 7 T | | 8 B | O | S | 9 S |
| O | | E | | W | | 10 H | E | R | E | | R | | | E |
| W | | 11 V | O | I | C | E | | 12 M | A | 13 N | A | 14 G | E | R |
| 15 S | E | E | | M | | M | | | | O | | R | | V |
| | | 16 N | A | M | E | | 17 S | 18 U | N | S | H | A | D | E |
| 19 H | 20 O | T | | I | | 21 S | | N | | E | | P | | |
| 22 A | N | Y | | 23 N | A | P | K | I | N | | 24 D | E | 25 A | 26 L |
| 27 I | T | | | G | | E | | O | | 28 S | | | 29 S | O |
| 30 L | O | 31 A | N | | 32 C | A | N | N | O | T | | 33 S | I | T |
| | | P | | 34 A | | K | | S | | A | | 35 H | A | S |
| 36 C | A | R | E | L | E | S | S | | 37 I | N | T | O | | |
| A | | O | | S | | | | 38 O | | D | | 39 R | U | 40 M |
| 41 T | I | N | 42 F | O | 43 I | 44 L | | 45 P | A | I | N | T | | E |
| C | | | O | | 46 T | I | 47 M | E | | N | | E | | S |
| 48 H | A | N | G | | 49 S | E | E | N | | 50 G | I | R | L | S |

**TEST 65:**

1. compartment
2. arrogance
3. candle
4. snow
5. gas
6. rice
7. furniture
8. button
9. week
10. Dollar
11. vase
12. length
13. books
14. pointed
15. to write
16. horse
17. East
18. orange
19. address

**TEST 66:**

1. Two men are working on a road.
2. One of them digs a hole.
3. The other immediately fills it up.
4. This happens a number of times.
5. A passer-by observes this happening.
6. He asks them why they're doing that and the men explain it to him.
7. "There are normally three of us."
8. "And what does the third guy do?" the passer-by wants to know.
9. "He puts the lanterns in the holes, but today he is ill."

**TEST 67:**

**1.** sing **2.** says **3.** just **4.** deal **5.** tap **6.** fun **7.** seize **8.** latest
**9.** soap **10.** news **11.** do **12.** ship **13.** danger **14.** great
**15.** another **16.** takes **17.** class **18.** green **19.** nice **20.** short

**TEST 68:**

| | | | | | | | | | | | | |
|---|---|---|---|---|---|---|---|---|---|---|---|---|
| | | | | | **G** | R | A | N | D | S | O | N |
| S | I | S | T | E | **R** | | | | | | | |
| | | | | | **A** | U | N | T | | | | |
| | | | | | **N** | I | E | C | E | | | |
| | | | | | **D** | A | U | G | H | T | E | R |
| | | | | | **M** | O | T | H | E | R | | |
| | | | | S | **O** | N | | | | | | |
| | | | | | **T** | W | I | N | S | | | |
| | | N | E | P | **H** | E | W | | | | | |
| | U | N | C | L | **E** | | | | | | | |
| F | A | T | H | E | **R** | | | | | | | |

**TEST 69:**

1. false
2. true
3. true
4. false
5. true
6. true
7. true
8. true
9. true
10. true
11. true
12. false
13. true
14. true
15. false
16. true
17. true
18. false
19. true
20. false

**TEST 70:**

**1.** got **2.** listen **3.** make **4.** meaning **5.** thousands **6.** sooner **7.** early **8.** elections **9.** ninety **10.** Dutch **11.** matter **12.** customs **13.** complaint **14.** speak **15.** this **16.** Spanish **17.** site

**TEST 71:**

1. export - import
2. love - hate
3. guest - host
4. heat - cold
5. depth - height
6. length - breadth
7. life - death
8. hunger - thirst
9. poverty - riches
10. student - teacher
11. friend - enemy
12. summer - winter
13. heaven - hell
14. angel - devil
15. day - night
16. west - east
17. minority - majority
18. lies - truth
19. marriage - divorce
20. happiness - sadness

**TEST 72:**

| | | | | | | | | | | | | | | |
|---|---|---|---|---|---|---|---|---|---|---|---|---|---|---|
| [1] G | A | [2] S | ■ | [3] I | R | [4] I | S | [5] H | ■ | [6] I | N | [7] D | I | [8] A |
| L | ■ | W | ■ | N | ■ | T | ■ | E | ■ | M | ■ | A | ■ | G |
| [9] A | H | E | A | D | ■ | [10] S | [11] H | A | R | P | E | N | E | R |
| S | ■ | E | ■ | I | ■ | ■ | [12] A | T | ■ | O | ■ | C | ■ | E |
| [13] S | I | T | U | A | T | [14] E | D | ■ | [15] G | R | E | E | C | E |
| ■ | ■ | C | ■ | N | | L | ■ | [16] B | ■ | T | ■ | ■ | ■ | M |
| [17] P | O | O | L | ■ | [18] B | E | [19] F | O | R | E | ■ | [20] P | I | E |
| O | ■ | R | ■ | [21] A | ■ | [22] V | A | T | ■ | D | ■ | R | ■ | N |
| [23] I | N | N | ■ | [24] P | R | E | T | T | Y | ■ | [25] S | E | A | T |
| S | ■ | ■ | ■ | P | ■ | N | ■ | L | ■ | [26] P | ■ | P | ■ | ■ |
| [27] O | P | [28] E | N | E | R | ■ | [29] L | E | M | O | N | A | D | [30] E |
| N | ■ | X | ■ | A | ■ | [31] S | O | ■ | ■ | W | ■ | R | ■ | I |
| [32] I | N | T | E | R | C | I | T | [33] Y | ■ | [34] D | O | I | N | G |
| N | ■ | R | ■ | E | ■ | Z | ■ | E | ■ | E | ■ | N | ■ | H |
| [35] G | R | A | N | D | ■ | [36] E | N | T | E | R | ■ | [37] G | E | T |

**TEST 73:**

**1.** number **2.** comfort **3.** speak **4.** understand **5.** train **6.** shoes **7.** small **8.** attend **9.** loss **10.** break **11.** general **12.** get **13.** extent **14.** metres **15.** regards **16.** there **17.** goes **18.** step **19.** minutes **20.** glass

**TEST 74:**

**1.** UNDERSHIRT **2.** SUSPENDERS **3.** TIGHTS **4.** BRA(SSIERE) **5.** PULLOVER **6.** OVERCOAT **7.** TROUSERS **8.** SANDALS **9.** COSTUME **10.** SWEATER **11.** JACKET **12.** GLOVES **13.** BLOUSE **14.** BOOTS **15.** SOCKS **16.** APRON **17.** SHOES **18.** DRESS **19.** SCARF **20.** SKIRT **21.** VEST **22.** SHIRT **23.** SLIP **24.** BELT **25.** SUIT **26.** CAP **27.** TIE **28.** HAT

**TEST 75:**

1. bank
2. books
3. match
4. aquarium
5. to smoke
6. Denmark
7. bald
8. to whisper
9. divorce
10. blood
11. Catholic
12. daily
13. fuel
14. interest
15. single
16. to see
17. drunk
18. many
19. day
20. end

**TEST 76:**

**1.** speaking **2.** hurry **3.** fried **4.** put **5.** Step **6.** keep **7.** repaired **8.** call **9.** from **10.** contract **11.** name **12.** when **13.** calculation **14.** Hold **15.** pardon **16.** school **17.** number **18.** first **19.** successful **20.** fortunately

**TEST 77:**

1. true
2. false
3. true
4. false
5. false
6. true
7. true
8. false
9. false
10. false
11. true
12. true
13. false
14. true
15. true
16. true
17. true
18. false
19. true
20. false

**TEST 78:**

**1.** thank **2.** just **3.** train **4.** stop **5.** from **6.** paper **7.** prefer **8.** dig **9.** ticket **10.** hard **11.** reckon **12.** everything **13.** in **14.** repaired **15.** abroad **16.** gone **17.** are **18.** saying **19.** born **20.** good

**TEST 79:**

| | | | | | | | | | | | | | | |
|---|---|---|---|---|---|---|---|---|---|---|---|---|---|---|
| 1 E | A | 2 T | | 3 T | A | 4 P | | 5 E | A | 6 R | R | 7 I | N | 8 G |
| Y | | 9 A | G | O | | O | | L | | E | | T | | E |
| 10 E | G | G | | 11 I | N | S | T | E | A | D | | 12 S | 13 I | T |
| B | | | | L | | T | | C | | U | | | N | |
| 14 R | O | 15 B | B | E | D | | 16 S | T | O | C | K | 17 I | N | 18 G |
| O | | E | | T | | 19 T | | R | | E | | N | | E |
| 20 W | A | T | E | R | P | R | O | O | F | | 21 E | V | I | L |
| | | W | | Y | | A | | N | | 22 J | | O | | |
| 23 C | R | E | W | | 24 I | N | V | I | T | A | T | I | O | 25 N |
| A | | E | | 26 E | | S | | C | | P | | C | | A |
| 27 P | 28 E | N | K | N | I | F | E | | 29 S | A | F | E | S | T |
| | Y | | | T | | E | | 30 I | | N | | | | U |
| 31 B | E | 32 T | | 33 E | A | R | A | C | H | E | | 34 P | E | R |
| A | | I | | R | | E | | E | | 35 S | E | E | | A |
| 36 D | R | E | S | S | E | D | | 37 D | Y | E | | 38 A | L | L |

**TEST 80:**

BRUS**H**
SO**A**P
SPO**N**GE
POW**D**ER
LIPSTIC**K**
TOW**E**L
SCISSO**R**S
**C**OMB
MOUT**H**WASH
M**I**RROR
TW**E**EZERS
PER**F**UME

**TEST 81:**

1. bride - groom
2. husband - wife
3. grandfather - grandmother
4. son - daughter
5. brother - sister
6. uncle - aunt
7. nephew - niece
8. widower - widow
9. gentleman - lady
10. grandson - granddaughter
11. morning - evening
12. war - peace
13. old age - youth
14. departure - arrival
15. patient - doctor
16. entrance - exit

**TEST 82:**

**1.** lot **2.** arm **3.** cheques **4.** duty **5.** capacity **6.** day **7.** lend **8.** truth **9.** shipment **10.** vicinity **11.** from **12.** park **13.** injured **14.** insured **15.** great **16.** bottom **17.** after **18.** list **19.** rather **20.** mail

**TEST 83:**

1. sunset
2. China
3. son
4. nest
5. painting
6. poet
7. team
8. painter
9. sweet
10. aunt
11. sometimes
12. read
13. Asia
14. Europe
15. quiet
16. nutcracker
17. young
18. vegetable

**TEST 84:**

| | | | | | | | | | | | | | | |
|---|---|---|---|---|---|---|---|---|---|---|---|---|---|---|
| 1 A | G | 2 A | I | 3 N | S | 4 T | ■ | 5 I | N | 6 S | T | 7 A | N | 8 T |
| R | ■ | G | ■ | E | ■ | O | ■ | N | ■ | T | ■ | L | ■ | H |
| 9 T | W | O | ■ | 10 C | R | O | A | T | I | A | ■ | 11 L | I | E |
| I | ■ | ■ | ■ | K | ■ | K | ■ | R | ■ | T | ■ | ■ | ■ | A |
| 12 C | A | 13 S | T | L | E | ■ | 14 D | O | C | U | M | 15 E | N | T |
| L | ■ | T | ■ | A | ■ | 16 P | ■ | D | ■ | E | ■ | A | ■ | R |
| 17 E | U | R | O | C | H | E | Q | U | E | ■ | 18 F | R | E | E |
| ■ | ■ | A | ■ | E | ■ | D | ■ | C | ■ | 19 N | ■ | L | ■ | ■ |
| 20 P | I | N | K | ■ | 21 T | E | L | E | V | I | S | I | O | 22 N |
| R | ■ | G | ■ | 23 P | ■ | S | ■ | D | ■ | N | ■ | E | ■ | A |
| 24 O | M | E | L | E | T | T | E | ■ | 25 L | E | A | R | N | T |
| C | ■ | ■ | ■ | N | ■ | R | ■ | 26 R | ■ | T | ■ | ■ | ■ | U |
| 27 E | A | 28 T | ■ | 29 C | H | I | N | E | S | E | ■ | 30 W | A | R |
| S | ■ | O | ■ | I | ■ | A | ■ | N | ■ | E | ■ | H | ■ | A |
| 31 S | W | O | L | L | E | N | ■ | 32 T | I | N | F | O | I | L |

**TEST 85:**

**1.** miss **2.** understand **3.** switch **4.** gloves **5.** country **6.** well **7.** savings **8.** weakness **9.** course **10.** work **11.** ground **12.** afternoon **13.** fall **14.** hospital **15.** next **16.** step **17.** left **18.** late **19.** wood **20.** good

**TEST 86:**

1. Money makes the world go round.
2. Never look a gift horse in the mouth.
3. No man is a prophet in his own country.
4. No rose without a thorn.
5. No sweet without sweat.
6. Old love never dies.
7. One does not wash one's dirty linen in public.
8. One hand washes the other.
9. One swallow does not make a summer.
10. Opportunity makes a thief.
11. Opposites attract.

12. Poverty is no sin.
13. Practice makes perfect.
14. Revenge is sweet.
15. Speak of the devil, and he is bound to appear.
16. Speech is silver but silence is golden.
17. Strike while the iron is hot.
18. The apple never falls far from the tree.
19. The bigger they are, the harder they fall.
20. The early bird catches the worm.

**TEST 87:**

1. Brazil
2. to see
3. tablecloth
4. modern
5. to freeze
6. Hungary
7. to cook
8. to burn
9. solid
10. month
11. fruit
12. sad
13. war
14. fish
15. hot
16. monk
17. melody
18. fun

**TEST 88:**

**1.** Make **2.** probably **3.** Sorry **4.** know **5.** enough **6.** chicken **7.** right **8.** more **9.** learn **10.** Open **11.** sold **12.** old **13.** cake **14.** tomorrow **15.** pace **16.** accept **17.** condition **18.** luggage **19.** letters **20.** Good

**TEST 89:**

**1.** ALBANIA **2.** AUSTRIA **3.** BELGIUM **4.** BOSNIA **5.** BULGARIA **6.** CROATIA **7.** CYPRUS **8.** DENMARK **9.** FINLAND **10.** FRANCE **11.** GERMANY **12.** GREECE **13.** HUNGARY **14.** ICELAND **15.** IRELAND **16.** LUXEMBOURG **17.** NETHERLANDS **18.** NORWAY **19.** POLAND **20.** PORTUGAL **21.** ROMANIA **22.** RUSSIA **23.** SLOVAKIA **24.** SLOVENIA **25.** SPAIN **26.** SWEDEN **27.** SWITZERLAND **28.** TURKEY **29.** YUGOSLAVIA

**TEST 90:**

1. hardworking - lazy
2. large / big - small
3. fat - thin
4. slow - fast
5. beautiful - ugly
6. near - far
7. dark - light
8. expensive - cheap
9. intelligent - stupid
10. white - black
11. soft - hard
12. many - few
13. alive - dead
14. exciting - boring
15. low - high
16. northern - southern
17. short - long
18. ill - healthy
19. single - married
20. right - left

**TEST 91:**

**1.** business **2.** How **3.** well **4.** at **5.** coat **6.** cross **7.** problem **8.** deserved **9.** pieces **10.** speak **11.** television **12.** into **13.** created **14.** there **15.** forbidden **16.** Turn **17.** bill **18.** holiday **19.** breath **20.** mood

**TEST 92:**

A young man in a French town claimed he was better at household chores than his wife. So she left him. He had to take care of things on his own. He learnt to iron, cook, clean and wash. One day he wanted to get rid of a particularly problematic stain on his clothes. He remembered that his mother had told him that gasoline cleans exceptionally well. So, he poured gasoline instead of washing powder into the washing machine. Then he went shopping. When he returned, his apartment had disappeared. A spark in the machine had caused an explosion which had burnt down the whole apartment. The stain was also gone.

**TEST 93:**

The lady who had the maximum number of children in Germany lived about 500 years ago. Her tombstone states that she gave birth to 38 boys and 15 girls, a total of 53 babies. This is not a high number when compared to a Russian farmer's wife who is supposed to have had 69 children, almost all of whom were born as quadruplets, triplets or twins. It is not known how many of them survived.

**TEST 94:**

**1.** directory **2.** allowed **3.** an **4.** cheque **5.** customers **6.** damaged **7.** skin **8.** Right **9.** working **10.** as **11.** seventy **12.** much **13.** help **14.** order **15.** sorry **16.** tomorrow **17.** anything **18.** Christmas **19.** anybody

**TEST 95:**

1. participants
2. Romania
3. colour
4. people
5. speech
6. blue
7. hate
8. calculate
9. penguin
10. beverage
11. roof
12. paint
13. chemical
14. floor
15. fish
16. intelligence
17. art
18. economic
19. cars
20. Slovakia

**TEST 96:**

**1.** WINDSURFING **2.** VOLLEYBALL **3.** WRESTLING **4.** BILLIARDS **5.** BADMINTON **6.** SWIMMING **7.** SHOOTING **8.** HURDLING **9.** HANDBALL **10.** FOOTBALL **11.** SAILING **12.** GLIDING **13.** BOWLING **14.** FENCING **15.** SKATING **16.** SKIING **17.** TENNIS **18.** DIVING **19.** ROWING **20.** RIDING **21.** KARATE **22.** HOCKEY **23.** BOXING **24.** CHESS **25.** POLO **26.** JUDO **27.** GOLF

**TEST 97:**

**1.** nine **2.** discussion **3.** without **4.** in **5.** first **6.** think **7.** night **8.** country **9.** piece **10.** breakdown **11.** roll **12.** can **13.** has **14.** bear **15.** banks **16.** pretending **17.** languages **18.** store **19.** clock **20.** way

**TEST 98:**

1. The exception proves the rule.
2. The leopard cannot change its spots.
3. The love of money is the root of all evil.
4. The road to hell is paved with good intentions.
5. The shoemaker's son always goes barefoot.
6. The sun shines upon all alike.
7. The tree is known by its fruit.
8. There are two sides to everything.
9. Time is money.
10. To err is human.
11. Too many cooks spoil the broth.
12. We all have our cross to bear.
13. Well begun is half done.
14. When in Rome, do as the Romans do.
15. When the cat's away the mice will play.
16. Where there is smoke there's fire.
17. Where there's a will there's a way.
18. You can't see the forest for the trees.
19. You can't have your cake and eat it.
20. You can't make an omelette without breaking eggs.

**TEST 99:**

**1.** whisper **2.** bellow **3.** drink **4.** speak **5.** snore **6.** smile **7.** laugh **8.** cough **9.** spit **10.** sing **11.** suck **12.** call **13.** kiss **14.** chew **15.** yawn **16.** blow **17.** bite **18.** eat

**TEST 100:**

**1.** fish **2.** directions **3.** blocked **4.** took **5.** insurance **6.** look **7.** wants **8.** receipt **9.** brother **10.** leg **11.** comfortable **12.** touch **13.** find **14.** connected **15.** matters **16.** tell **17.** boring **18.** translation **19.** temper **20.** soon